A Whirlwind in Dublin

Contributions in Drama and Theatre Studies
Series Editor: Joseph Donohue

American Popular Entertainment: Papers and Proceedings of the Conference on the History of American Popular Entertainment
Myron Matlaw, editor

George Frederick Cooke: Machiavel of the Stage
Don B. Wilmeth

Greek Theatre Practice
J. Michael Walton

Gordon Craig's Moscow *Hamlet:* A Reconstruction
Laurence Senelick

Theatrical Touring and Founding in North America
L. W. Conolly, editor

Bernhardt and the Theatre of Her Time
Eric Salmon, editor

Revolution in the Theatre: French Romantic Theories of Drama
Barry V. Daniels

Serf Actor: The Life and Career of Mikhail Shchepkin
Laurence Senelick

Musical Theatre in America: Papers and Proceedings of the Conference on the Musical Theatre in America
Glenn Loney, editor
The American Society for Theatre Research, The Sonneck Society, and the Theatre Library Association, joint sponsors

Garrick Claims the Stage: Acting as Social Emblem in Eighteenth-Century England
Leigh Woods

A Whirlwind in Dublin
The Plough and the Stars Riots

Edited by
Robert G. Lowery

Contributions in Drama and Theatre Studies, Number 11

Greenwood Press
Westport, Connecticut ● London, England

Library of Congress Cataloging in Publication Data
Main entry under title:

A Whirlwind in Dublin.

(Contributions in drama and theatre studies,
ISSN 0163-3821 ; no 11)
    Bibliography: p.
    Includes index.
    1. O'Casey, Sean, 1880-1964. Plough and the stars.
2. Dublin (Dublin)—Riots, 1926. 3. Abbey Theatre—
History. 4. Theater—Ireland—Dublin (Dublin)—History—
20th century. I. Lowery, Robert G., 1941-
II. Series.
PR6029.C33P638   1984   822'.912   83-22652
ISBN 0-313-23764-6 (lib. bdg.)

Copyright © 1984 by Robert G. Lowery

All rights reserved. No portion of this book may be
reproduced, by any process or technique, without the
express written consent of the publisher.

Library of Congress Catalog Card Number: 83-22652
ISBN: 0-313-23764-6
ISSN: 0163-3821

First published in 1984

Greenwood Press
A division of Congressional Information Service, Inc.
88 Post Road West
Westport, Connecticut 06881

Printed in the United States of America

10 9 8 7 6 5 4 3 2 1

Copyright Acknowledgments

Permission to reproduce material from the following sources is gratefully acknowledged.

Rosie Redmond's song (end of Act II) from "THE PLOUGH AND THE STARS by Sean O'Casey" in *THREE PLAYS by Sean O'Casey*. First Edition of *The Plough and the Stars,* 1926; First issued in St. Martin's Library, 1957. By permission of St. Martin's Press, Inc. New York (U.S. Rights). Permission covering British Commonwealth and Canadian rights was granted by Macmillan Accounts and Administration Ltd.

Reprinted with permission of Macmillan Publishing Company from THE LETTERS OF SEAN O'CASEY, Volume I: 1910-41, edited by David Krause. Copyright © 1975 by Macmillan Publishing Company.

From JOSEPH HOLLOWAY'S ABBEY THEATRE: A SELECTION FROM HIS UNPUBLISHED JOURNAL, "IMPRESSIONS OF A DUBLIN PLAYGOER," Edited by Robert Hogan and Michael J. O'Neill. Copyright © 1967 by Southern Illinois University Press. Reprinted by permission of Southern Illinois University Press.

Articles from THE IRISH TIMES: "The Plough and the Stars, Mr Sean O'Casey's New Play," 9 February 1926; "Abbey Theatre Scenes," 12 February 1926; and "Cant and Facts" (editorial), 13 February 1926, by permission of The Irish Times Limited.

"New Play Resented, Last Night's Scenes in the Abbey Theatre," 12 February 1926, by permission of the EVENING HERALD (Dublin).

"Sean O'Casey's New Play 'The Plough and the Stars'," 9 February 1926; and " 'The Plough and the Stars,' Author Replies to Republican's Charges, A Piquant Debate," 2 March 1926, by permission of the IRISH INDEPENDENT.

Stephen Gwynn Review, by permission of THE OBSERVER (London).

Extracts from LADY GREGORY'S JOURNALS by permission of Colin Smythe Limited and the Lady Gregory Estate.

Extracts from THE LETTERS OF W. B. YEATS, by permission of Michael and Anne Yeats.

Every reasonable effort has been made to trace the owners of copyright materials in this book, but in some instances this has proved impossible. The publishers will be glad to receive information leading to more complete acknowledgments in subsequent printings of the book and in the meantime extend their apologies for any omissions.

To the memory of

Angela Newman and Bill Foley,

Abbey Theatre

The play has raised something of a whirlwind in Dublin.

—Letter from Sean O'Casey to
Sara Allgood, 23 February 1926

Contents

Preface	xiii
Introduction	3
1. The Temple Shaken	9
2. The Whirlwind	21
3. *Vox Litteratoris*	57
Notes	109
Appendix: Biographical Notes	113
Suggestions for Further Reading	117
Index	119

Preface

Sean O'Casey's characterization of the riots surrounding the first production of *The Plough and the Stars* as a "whirlwind" was also a symbolic description of the play's impact on a broad spectrum of Irish society. The purpose of this book is to demonstrate that impact by presenting representative selections from the writings of those who were affected by, as well as from those who generated, the whirlwind; these selections are taken from independent journals, Dublin and London newspapers, and letters and memoirs of the central figures in the controversy. This variety of sources was chosen to balance conventional writings from newspapers which are in general representative, individually, of the editorial policy of the paper and, collectively, of a wealthy and powerful elite within a society.

Few of the documents have been edited—there is always a precarious danger in editing historical documents—though their time sequence has been altered in some cases in the interest of continuity. Documents are able to relate only what was written and reported. Readers should decide for themselves what actually occurred.

In order to present a broader perspective on what O'Casey so aptly described as "a whirlwind in Dublin," I have chosen to begin the examination of the controversy considerably before the 8 February 1926 premiere of the play.

A Whirlwind in Dublin

Introduction

> O'Casey is considered by many the only Irish playwright who can thus far compare with John M. Synge, although it is difficult to discover an adequate basis on which to judge them together.
> —Curtis Canfield, *Plays of the Irish Renaissance* (1929)

The riots surrounding the 1926 productions of *The Plough and the Stars* are invariably compared with similar disturbances of the 1907 production of John M. Synge's play *The Playboy of the Western World.* There is too much surface similarity to be ignored. Certainly the central figures of the *Plough* controversy were aware of the parallels: William Butler Yeats* invoked them in his famous speech at the Abbey; Lady Augusta Gregory* fretted over the disturbing possibilities before anything happened; and news stories did not mention one without mentioning the other. Those who protested against the *Plough* considered the occasion another insult to the Irish people in the tradition of the *Playboy*; and those who condemned the protesters pointed to the shameful tradition of theatre protest, a tradition which definitely included the *Playboy.*

Few can deny that certain essential similarities existed between the two occasions. In both instances a "disgraceful" play appeared on the stage of the Abbey, Ireland's national theatre, offending a

---

*An asterisk following a name in the text section of the book indicates that biographical information on that person is provided in the Appendix.

sizable segment of the audience. In each case the playwright was accused of defaming Ireland's national honor, good name, and people. In both examples the protests began in the theatre and disrupted the play; they spread to the Dublin newspaper columns and involved a number of Ireland's intellectuals and writers as well as several ordinary letter-to-the-editor writers.

The protesters in each case were similar. In each instance the police were called to eject the disrupters, who sang the same songs and shouted the same slogans in 1926 as they did in 1907. Both groups accused Synge and O'Casey of creating "stage Irishmen" and of distorting reality. Each group, particularly the letter writers, demanded that Ireland apply the same standards of dramatic expression as England and the United States did—meaning that since neither of those countries would tolerate such an insult, why should Ireland? Further, one finds that in addition to turning their wrath against the dramatists, the protesters cast a major portion of the blame for disgracing Ireland on the directors of the Abbey Theatre.

The defenders of the plays used similar logic in their rebuttals. Both plays, they said, were examples of drama at its finest. The characters in the plays, while distorted, were exaggerated only in the best tradition of dramatic license and were not meant to be accurate portrayals from everyday life. Moreover, said the defenders, a national theatre could not be either national or a theatre without freedom of artistic expression.

Finally, there were miscellaneous parallels. For example, in each case the Abbey players resolved to continue the production despite threats and dangers, and in each case several people maintained that while they did not like the plays, those concerned had the right to see them performed and to have them receive a fair hearing.

There were, however, major differences between the two occasions. First, the historical settings were nineteen years apart. The Ireland of Synge was not the Ireland of O'Casey. By 1926 the country had been through a psyche-shattering culmination of political and social events which claimed the flower of a generation as victims. Within a space of nine years (1913-1922), the Dublin working class was crushed, leaders were executed, cities and towns were burned and terrorized, and documents and treaties were bandied about while a Kafkaesque civil war raged.

The Ireland of Synge had none of this except in the minds of the destined few. The trauma of Synge's Ireland was from divisions created by the fall of Charles Stewart Parnell,* Ireland's Home Rule champion in the British Parliament. Though this event was not without major impact, the event itself passed without assassinations, death and destruction, or new gravesites. Synge's Ireland remembered the 1898 centenary celebrations of the United Irishmen and the antirecruiting campaign of the Boer War. Trade union leader James Larkin* was in Belfast and a major strike uniting Protestant and Catholic workers was only months away. Most of all, though, this Ireland had various gradations of Irish-Irelanders. If the Ireland of 1907 did not have newfound martyrs, it did have enthusiasm in its search for Daniel Corkery's hidden Ireland, for W. B. Yeats's Celtic twilight, and for Douglas Hyde's Gaelic League. Societies and clubs formed throughout the country to study a language, a literature, and a dream. The infant Abbey Theatre, only three years old, was immersed in a thousand-year-old revival, and the peasant dramas brought an elegant simplicity to the stage.

The essential difference, then, between the two periods was that the Ireland of 1907 was going somewhere; the Ireland of 1926 had been there. The former had its head in the clouds; the latter had crashed to earth. In 1907 there was life; in 1926 there were only martyrs.

The second major difference was in the plays themselves. Both plays dealt with similar socioeconomic groups: Synge's peasants and O'Casey's working class. But O'Casey's drama had one thing that was absent from *Playboy*: a national shrine. O'Casey's use of the 1916 Rising (then being commemorated in its tenth year) was central to the protesters' anger. Rosie Redmond and Pegeen Mike were objectionable for puritanical reasons; Nora was unacceptable because she did not embody the image of Patrick Pearse's* "Mother" and because, according to the protesters, she disgraced the women of 1916. Further, it was one thing to show Christy Mahon as a rogue; Ireland was full of that type. But it was something else to show Jack Clitheroe and others as "cowards," especially during an event considered by many as almost equivalent to Lourdes.

Finally, there were differences in the chronology and intensity of the protests. Though both premieres were sold out, the *Playboy* audience dwindled substantially after the first night. Reviewers wrote of a "very thin" house of "small dimensions." The *Plough,* however, was booked solid for the week and played to full houses for the entire run. The *Playboy* riots began on the first night and continued with growing intensity for several nights. But the *Plough* disturbances did not occur until the fourth night (although there were a few minor catcalls during the second and third performances). For this reason the newspapers in 1926 were unable to fan the discontent as they had done in 1907. During *Playboy,* violent exchanges of opinions appeared in the press immediately following the first night. But the *Plough* gained a respite and large numbers were able to see and judge the play without being influenced by the controversy. Moreover, in 1907 the protesters were led by men who did considerable damage to the Abbey's interior. In 1926 the protesters, mainly women, did more disrupting than damage.

There was, then, both similarity and difference between the disturbances surrounding the *Playboy* and the *Plough*. Both situations were as much a result of the circumstances surrounding the plays as of the contents of the plays, yet the circumstances and contents were different. The protesters adopted similar methods and rationalizations for their actions, though their actions varied in degree, direction, and chronology.

Between the years of *Playboy* and *Plough*, the Abbey Theatre's fortunes fluctuated. Lady Gregory recorded a decline dating from 1915, a recovery in 1918, but another serious reversal after the civil war. By 1923 the Abbey was dependent on foreign tours to break even and, in that year, requested (unsuccessfully) a remittance of taxes from the government. In 1924, the theatre directors mortgaged their building for the first time to pay off overdrafts, and it was estimated that a loss of £4000 had been incurred since 1912. Despite this, there was breathing room, with some small discretionary funds available, but barely enough for more than minor repairs.

It is not difficult to imagine the fate of the Abbey had O'Casey not appeared. Few now doubt that it was his plays *The Shadow of a Gunman* (1923) and *Juno and the Paycock* (1924) which literally saved the Abbey from bankruptcy. Lady Gregory recorded that they were "immense" successes and, more often than not, filled the theatre with paying customers.

Perhaps because of this, the Abbey was finally awarded a small subsidy (£850) in 1925 by the Irish government, not half of what was requested and only a fraction of what was needed, but it was a start. With the subsidy and with O'Casey's plays drawing well and his promise of a new and more ambitious drama to come, the future looked bright.

1
The Temple Shaken

> Mr. O'Casey, it is said, wrote the "Plough and the Stars" in three weeks. What delayed him?
> —*Dublin Opinion*

The first suggestions that *The Plough and the Stars* was to be more than just another play came in two letters from O'Casey to Lady Gregory in 1924, eighteen months before the premiere. By July 1924 the play already had a name, O'Casey calling it "my most ambitious play, 'The Plough and the Stars.' " By October he was "anxious to start work on 'The Plough and the Stars' which, dealing with Easter Week, will bring to our Remembrance 'old unhappy far off days, & battles long ago!' "[1] Nine months later, on 12 August 1925, O'Casey recorded that the play was complete, and he submitted it to the Abbey directors: Lennox Robinson,* George O'Brien,* W. B. Yeats, and Lady Gregory. Coincidentally, O'Casey was preparing to visit Lady Gregory at this time, having been invited by her the previous winter. O'Casey arrived in Coole Park on 22 August and the whirlwind began to form. Lady Gregory wrote in her journals:

> Aug. 23 (Coole). Casey arrived yesterday. His play, *The Plough and the Stars*, had come in the morning with a letter from Lennox Robinson saying he and W. B. Yeats liked it. I slipped away after dinner and read the first act to myself, and

finding it so good, I took it to the library and read it to Jack [?] and his wife, (and the author) and they liked it, a fine opening but tragic. He has been working on it for thirteen months and is tired and glad of a rest, his delight in the country as great as ever, for he still lives in his tenement room.

Sept. 2. [Michael] Dolan* writes objecting to *The Plough and the Stars.* "At any time I would think twice before having anything to do with it. The language is—to use an Abbey phrase—'beyond the beyonds.' The song at the end of the second act, sung by the 'girl-of-the-street,' is impossible. . . ."

Yeats says Casey said about the song that must be removed from the play, "Yes. It's a pity. It would offend thousands. But it ought to be there."[2]

The "impossible" song that "would offend thousands" was indeed a bawdy tune, given the times. Yet it was also a delightful little verse:

> I once had a lover, a tailor, but he could do nothin' for me,
> An' then I fell in with a sailor as strong an' wild as th' sea.
> We cuddled an' kissed with devotion, till th' night from th' mornin' had fled;
> An' there, to our joy, a bright bouncin' boy,
> Was dancin' a jig in th' bed!
>
> Dancin' a jig in th' bed, an' bawlin' for butther an' bread.
> An' there, to our joy, a bright bouncin' boy
> Was dancin' a jig in th' bed.[3]

The song was summarily cut out of the play.

Each director had his own opinion of the play. According to Lady Gregory, O'Brien's impression was initially favorable: "As to our new Director, George O'Brien, he had written me Aug. 26th, 'I read O'Casey's play yesterday. While I have no pretension to be an expert dramatic critic, I feel quite safe in saying that I think it excellent.' " But Dolan, who had been with the Abbey longer than O'Brien, was worried:

Now, Lady Gregory, I respectfully beg of you to pause and think what it will mean. As you know we cannot afford to take risks, especially at the present moment. The theatre is booming at the present and unfortunately there are too many people who are sorry that such is the case. We don't want to give them anything to grasp at. . . .

I consulted Mr. George O'Brien about the whole play. He said he had written to you a general benediction about it, but agreed with me that there is a huge difference between reading a play at home and hearing it from a stage. I don't want to protest too much, especially as O'Casey and myself had a heated argument about the production of Man and Superman.[4] I can assure you the latter has nothing to do with it. As a matter of fact, when and if it is read to the company I feel there will be a real difficulty in getting them to play in it. . . .[5]

O'Brien began to have second thoughts about the play (probably from having talked to Dolan). In September, he and Yeats (with Lennox Robinson) exchanged letters:

5 September 1925

Dear Mr. Yeats,

I have read O'Casey's new play and am convinced that it would be quite as successful as any of his others if produced. There are, however, certain particulars in which I think the play in its present form would seriously offend the audience and I think that it must be amended in certain respects before it can be staged.

The love scene between Clitheroe and his wife in Act I does not read true, and I am inclined to think that it could be easily improved. But even if it is let stand as it is there are a couple of phrases which I think would annoy the audience. These are:—

"You can; come on, put your leg against mine—there."
"Little rogue of th' white breast."

(Act I, p. 19)

My most serious objection is to Act II where, in my opinion, the introduction of the prostitute is quite unnecessary to the action. Of course the mere introduction of a prostitute as a character in the play is not in itself objectionable but I think that the character as presented by Mr. O'Casey is objectionable. The lady's professional side is unduly emphasised in her actions and conversation and I think that the greater part of this scene should be re-written. In view of this general objection I shall not trouble you with the particular phrases in this act to which I take exception as they are very numerous and I think could not possibly be allowed to stand. The song at the end is an example of what I mean.

My only other objections to the play are to particular phrases and modes of expression which could easily be omitted or altered without in any way interfering with the main structure of the play. I will go through these seriatim.

(1). The words "Jesus" "Jasus" and "Christ" occur frequently (e.g. Act I p. 12, Act III p. 8, Act IV, pp. 15 and 18). These words used as expletives would certainly give offence.

(2). On Act I p. 11 there is a speech "I'll leave you to th' day when th' all-pitiful, all-merciful, all-lovin' God'll be rievin' an' roastin' you; tearin' an' tormentin' you; burnin' an' blastin' you!"

There are similar phrases to be found in Act III, p. 10 (near the top) and Act IV, p. 3 (at the bottom). These speeches would offend the audience and must be altered.

(3). On Act II, p. 10 the speeches of Bessie Burgess and Mrs. Gogan contain objectionable expressions which could be considerably toned down with advantage.

(4). The vituperative vocabulary of some characters occasionally runs away with itself. As examples of what I mean I would refer to the last words of The Covey before his exit on Act I, p. 17, the last two speeches on Act II, p. 16, and the last speech on Act III, p. 13. I think that the numerous references to "lowsers" and "lice" should be changed.

(5). The word "bitch" occurs on Act I, p. 15, Act III, p. 4, and Act IV, p. 17. I think this should be altered.

I think you will agree with me that the play would be improved if the foregoing suggestions were accepted, and hope that Mr. O'Casey can be prevailed on to take the same view. I do not think that any of these alterations will materially alter the main action of the play, which, while excellent in its conception and execution, could not possibly be produced in precisely its present form.

Yours sincerely,
George O'Brien[6]

Yeats and Lennox Robinson answered:

82 Merrion Square
Dublin
10 September 1925

Dear O'Brien,

We agree with you about Clitheroe and his wife, that love scene in the first act is most objectionable and, as you say, does not read true. What is wrong is that O'Casey is there writing about people whom he does not know, people he has only read about. We had both decided when we first read the play that he should be asked to try and modify these characters, bringing them within the range of his knowledge. When that is done the objectionable elements will lose their sentimentality and thereby their artistic offence. We decided that if he cannot do this that the dialogue would have to be greatly modified in rehearsal.

Now we come to the prostitute in Act 2; she is certainly necessary to the general action and idea as are the drunkards and wastrels. O'Casey is contrasting the ideal dream with the normal grossness of life and of that she is an essential part. It is no use putting her in if she does not express herself vividly and in character, if her "professional" side is not emphasised. Almost certainly a phrase here and there must be altered in rehearsal but the scene as a whole is admirable, one of the finest O'Casey has written. To eliminate any part of it on grounds that have nothing to do with dramatic literature would be to deny all our traditions.

The other passages you mention are the kind of thing which are dealt with in rehearsal by the producer (in almost every one of O'Casey's plays the dialogue here and there has been a little modified and he has never objected to our modifications) but we are inclined to think that the use of the word "bitch" in Act 4 is necessary. It occurs when Bessie on receiving her mortal wound turns furiously on the women whose delirium has brought it on her. The scene is magnificent and we are loath to alter a word of it.

If you do not feel that this letter entirely satisfies you we can have a Directors' meeting on the subject.

Yours sincerely,
(W. B. Yeats and Lennox Robinson)[7]

Lady Gregory recorded O'Brien's reaction:

George O'Brien wrote, Sept. 13th: "Dear Mr. Yeats and Lennox, Thanks very much for your letter from which I am glad to learn that you do not think my criticism of the play unreasonable. I appreciate your willingness to meet my objection and I take it that the offensive passages I mentioned will be changed. As regards Act II, I am in a certain amount of difficulty. I quite see your point that to eliminate any part of it on grounds that have nothing to do with dramatic literature would be to destroy all our traditions. I feel, however, that there are certain other considerations affecting the production to which it is, in a peculiar way, my duty to have regard. One of these is the possibility that the play might offend any section of public opinion so seriously as to provoke an attack on the Theatre of a kind that would endanger the continuance of the subsidy. Now I think that the play as it stands might easily provoke such an attack. Your statement that 'a phrase here and there must be altered in rehearsal' suggests that there may not be very much difference of opinion between us. If you would let me know the phrases or passages in Act II which you think should be changed, I would consider the scene as altered very carefully, might perhaps suggest some other minor changes, and in this way we would most probably reach a compromise. I hope you will not be annoyed at my insistence in my objection which is based altogether on my desire to be of service to the Theatre. Not being a dramatic author or critic, I feel that the only assistance of value I can render is by attempting to prevent the outbreak of a movement of hostility that would make it difficult or impossible for the Government to continue or to increase its subsidy. Yours, George O'Brien.'"[8]

To Lady Gregory, this was nothing less than a veiled threat, and there was no question what her decision would be:

> Our position is clear. If we have to choose between the subsidy and our freedom, it is our freedom we choose. And we must tell him [O'Brien] there was no condition attached to the subsidy, and though in connection with it another Director was suggested, . . . there was no word at all of his being a censor, but only to strengthen us on the financial side, none of us being good at money-matters or accounts.[9]

On 24-25 September, the Abbey directors had a meeting. From Lady Gregory's account it is evident that not all were in agreement as to *how* cuts in the play were to be made, but all did agree on the same deletions and modifications.

> Sept. 24. The Directors' meeting. Dr. O'Brien making his objections to the play: I, chiefly spokesman (by request), telling him [Ernest] Blythe had made no hint of appointing a censor. I told him of our old fights about *Countess Cathleen* (with the Catholic Church),[10] *Blanco Posnet* (with the Government),[11] Lord Aberdeen's efforts to get passages left out of the play (as now played in England), and my refusal (though there was no real threat of closing the Theatre). Yeats also spoke in the same sense. O'Brien sat up in his chair reiterating at intervals, "That song is objectionable." (We had already decided that it must go, but left it as a bone for him to gnaw at.) "And the word bitch," etc. We told him cuts are usually made in rehearsal, by producers and players, but that we had at the beginning told Casey the Clitheroe parts must be rewritten, etc., and at last got O'Brien to confess, "I had mistaken my position" (of censor). But he wants to see a rehearsal a little later. I then proposed (already arranged) that now we are four Directors we had better bring a rule of majority voting or we might come to a deadlock, two and two; and we

passed that resolution; the chairman to have a casting vote. It was a long meeting: I wished some artist could have looked in, Yeats and I so animated, Lennox Robinson so amused, George O'Brien sitting upright repeating, "That song must be left out!"

Sept. 25. Directors' meeting easy. O'Brien like a lamb, though after it he held [John] Perrin [secretary of the Abbey Theatre] to say, "I think Mr. Robinson has now given up that song."[12]. . .

O'Casey was aware of the consternation among the Abbey directors and of their efforts to tone down the language to a producible level. He was consulted about the changes and remained on good terms with them. However, he was equally concerned about the casting of the play. Excerpts from two letters to the Abbey actor Gabriel Fallon,* who had become O'Casey's good friend, written while the dramatist was at Coole, are indicative of the anxiety he felt:

. . . I am still very anxious about the Caste, & it's a pity I didn't read it to you & to Barry Fitzgerald,* before the Abbey opened, so as to get suggestions. I wonder ought I to chance young [Shelah] Richards* for the part of Nora? Or Ria Mooney? Which of the two would you suggest? I was thinking of Eileen Crowe* for the part of the "young daughter of the Digs." And [John P.] Stephenson for either the "figure in the window;" or for the part of Jack Clitheroe. . . .

. . . I'm not sure yet about Sheila Richards. What do you mean by a "good Producer"? I'm anxious that Lennox Robinson should produce the play. As soon as he returns to Dublin I'll ask him.

And "The figure at the window" is an important personage. The force of the 2nd Act depends upon this character, & if Stephenson plays Clitheroe, whom shall I get to play the figure? I have asked "JP" to give you the MM.S.[sic, for MS] to read. I hope you got it. If you have read it, you will understand why I am troubled, too, about the part of Mrs. Gogan. [Maureen] Delaney is too merry for the part, & [May]

Craig* is, I think impossible. I should choose myself, Helen Moloney; but I'm afraid that's almost out of the question.

Isn't it terrible that Peter Judge [F. J. McCormick*] should be content to constitute himself an echo? I'm thinking of writing to him telling him the play has passed, suggesting he should play "The Young Covey" & asking his opinion of the play.

What about yourself for the part of Peter [Flynn]? If you can't or won't do this then the Covey or Peter must be played by Stephenson or McCormick; each in either part, I think. . . .[13]

In October, O'Casey suffered a disappointment. Sara Allgood,* for whom the character Bessie Burgess was written, was to be in London in James Bernard Fagan's* production of *Juno and the Paycock*. Moreover, Gabriel Fallon, whom O'Casey wanted for the role of Peter Flynn, resigned from the Abbey company (though he eventually did play the part of Captain Brennan).

By the first of the year, though, the Abbey company was rehearsing the play. Rosie Redmond's song remained completely out, no attempt being made to alter it. (Indeed, it did not reappear in the script and Abbey productions until the late 1940s.) The love scene between Jack and Nora in Act I was modified and everyone seemed satisfied. However, more problems arose. Two of the players, Eileen Crowe and F. J. McCormick (recently married in December 1925), refused to speak some of their lines. O'Casey threatened to withdraw the play. On 9 January he met with Lady Gregory and Lennox Robinson during rehearsal. The meeting was recorded by Lady Gregory.

> Jan. 10. Yesterday to the Abbey, and saw part of a rehearsal of the *Plough and the Stars*—the public-house scene [Act II], it will go well, I think, a good deal of variety in different points of view. Then Sean O'Casey came in, as it was over, sat down beside me and said he was indignant; that Miss Crowe has refused to speak a certain sentence in the play, and he holds that she has no right to refuse any sentence the Directors have passed. Lennox Robinson came on to the

stage and O'Casey repeated this, very emphatically, even angrily. Lennox Robinson said it was usual for players to say if there was anything they might object to in my plays, and they had sometimes done so, a dialect word having sometimes a different meaning in town and country. And I said, after the first night of *Playboy*, Synge had given leave to the players to leave out anything they liked; it was I who went through the script with them and some words were struck out. So then I talked of other things.

I told this to Yeats later and his indignation was all against Miss Crowe; he wanted to ring up Lennox Robinson and insist on her saying the words lest other players should follow her lead. But I told him Sean O'Casey was coming to tea with me and I'd see what he said. But when he came he was much less excited. And the words Miss Crowe objects to are, "I had never a child that was not born within the border of the Ten Commandments," and this I heard her say in the rehearsal and it had certainly not struck me as offensive. So I don't know what will happen. It was like one of our storms in a teacup.[14]

Following the meeting, O'Casey wrote Lennox Robinson a letter.

10 January 1926

Dear Mr. Robinson,

I have carefully and (I hope) impartially re-read The Plough and the Stars, lingering thoughtfully over those passages that have irritated or shocked some of the members of the Caste, and I cannot admit into my mind any reason for either rejection or alteration.

Miss Crowe's hesitation over part of the dialogue of Mrs. Gogan seems to me to be inconsistent when I remember she was eager to play the central figure in [O'Casey's play] "Nannie's Night Out", which was as low (God help us) and, possibly lower, than the part of Mrs. Gogan.

Neither can I see any reason standing beside the objection to such words as Snotty, Bum, Bastard or Lowsey. To me it isnt timidity but cowardice that shades itself from them.

Lowsey is in "Paul Twyning"; is it to be allowed in that play and rejected in mine? Bastard in "The Devil's Discipline"† is said with all the savagery of a callous bigot to a young child: is the word to flourish in that play and wither in mine? Snotty is simply an expression for sarcastic or jeering.

The play itself is (in my opinion) a deadly compromise with the actual; it has been further modified by the Directors but I draw the line at a Vigilance Committee of the Actors.

I am sorry, but I'm not Synge; not even, I'm afraid, a reincarnation. Besides, things have happened since Synge: the war has shaken some of the respectability out of the heart of man; we have had our own changes, and the U.S.S.R. has fixed a new star in the sky. Were corrections of this kind to be suffered the work would be one of fear, for everyone would start a canonical pruning, (as a matter of fact Miss [Ria] Mooney has complained to me about the horror of the part) and impudent fear would dominate the place of quiet courage.

As I have said, these things have been deeply pondered, and under the circumstances, and to avoid further trouble, I prefer to withdraw the play altogether.

Sincerely yours,
Sean O'Casey[15]

With only three weeks left before opening night, the last cut in dialogue was made. Lady Gregory wrote:

> Jan. 16. . . . Miss Crowe having, after consultation with the priest, refused to say the words 'within the border of the Ten Commandments,' in her part, and McCormick has refused to say his 'No, I will not be called "snotty." ' Snotty in old English, according to Webster, is a 'mean, ugly person,' and quite innocent. Casey writes to withdraw his play. . . . We decided to let her husband leave out the word he objected to, as Miss Richards, who replied to him, means to use it.[16]

---

†O'Casey puns, rather than errs, on his use of Shaw's play, *The Devil's Disciple.*

O'Casey's play was no secret to Dubliners. Neither was the subject matter. On 12 January the *Irish Times* carried an article, " 'The Plough and the Stars': Mr. Sean O'Casey's New Play," which described its essentials. On 4 February, four days before opening night, Joseph Holloway,* the unofficial chronicler of the Dublin theatre scene, noted in his journal: "Dublin is agog about [O'Casey's] new play." Ten days before opening night, the Abbey was booked solid for the entire one-week run. On 7 February, Holloway attended the last rehearsal and recorded his impressions.

> Sunday, February 7. I attended the dress rehearsal of O'Casey's *The Plough and the Stars* at the Abbey, which didn't commence till after six o'clock and concluded some minutes after ten. The last act will save the play; the second I am of the opinion is quite unnecessary. On the whole, I imagine, as far as I can judge from such a performance, it is not nearly as interesting and gripping a piece as *Juno and the Paycock*. Will Shields [Barry Fitzgerald] was most indistinct in his utterance. May Craig was consistently good, and Shelah Richards promises to be a big success. I did not care for Maureen Delany, save in the final act into which she got the right note. . . . There are some moments of real drama in Act III. Act II was badly managed, the bar placed to one side, cut off from half the house. Ria Mooney's part, a prostitute, in Act II is quite unnecessary; and the incident in Act I about the naked female is lugged in for nastiness' sake alone.
>
> Robinson mostly reviewed the rehearsal from the pit, going up on stage every now and then to tell the players what he wanted them to do with this or that situation, and always giving them effective advice. . . . O'Casey was about on the stage between the acts and seated alone in the front row of the stalls, and later on with some of the players in the stalls. He seemed anxious. . . .[17]

2
The Whirlwind

> Sean O'Casey—The Answer to "Who Fears to Speak of Easter Week."
>
> —*Dublin Opinion*

Opening night of any major theatrical event is an occasion for celebration and festivities. Monday evening, 8 February 1926, was no exception. One journalist wrote of "the electricity in the air"; another called it "the high-water mark of public interest in the Abbey Theatre." All the notables were present, the audience was friendly and encouraging, and, according to the reviews, the Abbey players were in excellent form. Only scant attention was paid to the character Rosie Redmond, nobody commented on the Irish flag in the pub, and Sara Allgood wasn't really missed.

"It's a woman's play, a drama in which men must fight and women must weep," wrote the reviewer for the *Irish Times*, probably the only newspaper to withstand the coming hysteria. The reviewer was tremendously impressed with the personality of Bessie Burgess and the power of the dialogue:

"THE PLOUGH AND THE STARS"
MR. SEAN O'CASEY'S NEW PLAY

The high-water mark of public interest in the work of the Abbey Theatre was reached last night, when Mr. Sean

O'Casey's latest play, "The Plough and the Stars," had its first production.

Although it was well known that the house had been booked out many days ago, people who had not secured seats began to gather outside the theatre as early as four o'clock in the afternoon, in the hope that standing room in the back of the pit might be available. The first curtain went up with the packed theatre in a state of tense expectation, after each of the four acts there was a demonstration of approval, and when the end came the author received an ovation.

"The Plough and the Stars" is a tragedy of Dublin tenement life of the period of the Rebellion of Easter Week, 1916. It has no plot in the ordinary theatrical meaning of the word. It has not got even the flimsy thread of a story on which "Juno and the Paycock" is worked out, and yet, with all the shortcomings of a first performance, with the audience as well as the players in a condition of high tension, the play progressed to its inexorable climax without the interest flagging for a second.

Mr. O'Casey paints the people among whom he has lived until quite recently. While history is being made all around in scenes of death and destruction, these people live their lives as they have lived them all along—drab and shiftless, in middle age or abounding in hope and expectation in youth; and we know that when the last curtain has fallen, the world of existence will continue in the same tenement way. Mr. O'Casey's play is more than realism; it is naturalism—a faithful reproduction of what happened, with the truth of the picture apparent to the dullest imagination. Great events are outlined only in so far as they have had reactions on the lives of the men and women that Mr. O'Casey recreates.

The title of the play is derived from the flag adopted by James Connolly's "Citizen Army" of 1915 and 1916. The earthly implement of toil is idealised into the heavenly constellation. The author translates that idealisation into the misery that its pursuit involves. He hates human suffering and in incident after incident, just as they would naturally happen in such surroundings, he makes the audience feel that it was not worth it; that one drop of the milk of human kindness is worth more than the deepest draughts of the red wine of idealism. Time and again, that thought is forced home, now in the lines of broad comedy, again in biting sarcasm, and finally in racking tragedy.

Jack Clitheroe is a bricklayer and a commandant in the Citizen Army. He duly loves his young wife, whose ideas of refinement are above her tenement house surroundings. Urged largely by vanity, he takes his part in the rebellion, and is killed. Nora loses her first baby, and then her husband, and that dream of happiness is shattered.

Bessie Burgess is a street-hawker, one of the roughest of the rough. She dislikes Nora's high and mighty notions of superiority to her poor neighbors, and, with a son in the Dublin Fusiliers in France, she despises the "Shinners." Inside the coarse exterior is a great heart, and Bessie is shot dead while dragging the irresponsible Nora from a position of danger at the window.

It is a woman's play, a drama in which men must fight and women must weep. Poor little Mollser, the dying consumptive girl, closes the curtain of the first act:—"Is there no one with a tither of sense?" That phrase may be described as the *motif* of "The Plough and the Stars," the tragedy of the women. None of the men characters adds to the development of the play, except that they are part of the life that is pictured.

Miss Delany's Bessie is great acting of what is undoubtedly the most perfect stage personality that Mr. O'Casey has yet created. We do not except even the lovable "Juno." For acting to character, Miss Craig was the success of the night. Her presentation of the thriftless, careless, reckless, char-woman deserved all the praise that is required. Miss Mooney, the young actress already noted for her vitality, had a part to play that was in no way inviting but which she made an integral portion of the play. The introduction of Rosie Redmond, a street girl, was a risky thing on the part of the author, but with Miss Mooney portraying her we felt again that Mr. O'Casey was giving us Dublin life as it was lived. Miss Crowe's lady from Rathmines, lost in tenement land in the upset of the times, was a cameo of theatrical beauty. Miss [Kitty] Curling made a completely successful *debut* as the consumptive girl.

Of the men, Mr. Fitzgerald plays a "Captain Boyle" part,

conceived and carried through on a plane far above that of the genial old ruffian, so delightful in "Juno." He is as irresistible when merely doing nothing as when carrying through the comedy that makes the first two acts stage-fun of the best. In Mr. [Eric] Gorman and Mr. Dolan he has two splendid helpers. Even Mr. McCormick, with all his talent, cannot make a live man out of Jack Clitheroe, but Mr. [Arthur] Shields's acting of the wounded lieutenant is fine work. One of the many thrills that the audience experienced came from Mr. Stephenson's declamation of the speech by the platform orator outside the window of the public-house in the second act.

The play is remarkable for the sparkle of its dialogue, even when, as often happens, character after character has to speak long, drawn out sentences. When these miniature speeches have been trimmed a little, "The Plough and the Stars" will be a better work.[1]

The reviewer from the *Irish Independent* was also impressed with the first-night excitement and he, too, noticed the dominant role of O'Casey's women. However, this reviewer saw a different heroine—Nora:

SEAN O'CASEY'S NEW PLAY
"THE PLOUGH AND THE STARS"

Not since "Blanco Posnet" has an Abbey first night aroused as much excitement as the production of "The Plough and the Stars," and Mr. Shaw had the advantage that his play had been banned in England, and there was a sporting chance that Dublin Castle, at the eleventh hour, would enforce a censorship of its own.

For the rest of the week the bookings have broken all Abbey records, a proof that one at least of our dramatic prophets does not lack honour in his own country.

Preliminary trumpetings about a new play, though they may be good business from the management's point of view, are not always fair to the author. I suspect a good many people went to the Abbey last night under the impression that "The Plough and the Stars" was as far above "Juno and the Paycock" as that piece was on "Kathleen Listens In."

THE OLD METHOD

While I have little doubt that this drama of Easter Week will prove to be the most popular of Mr. O'Casey's works, I do not think that artistically it marks an advance. This feeling may be partly due to the fact that we are all familiar by now with Mr. O'Casey's method. In "The Plough and the Stars" the method can still spring surprises, and the author gets effects with his material that no one else could equal; but, roughly speaking, the tragedy conforms too closely to one's preconceived idea of the sort of play that one who has mastered the technique of "Juno" would make out of a theme like the Easter Rising.

In some respects, Mr. O'Casey has bettered his hand. No figure sticks out so incongruously as Davoren the supposed poet did in "The Gunman," or Bentham, the freak theosophist, in "Juno," and Mr. O'Casey no longer hampers himself with such dead theatrical lumber as the legacy that is the fount and source of Captain Boyle's misfortunes. In "The Plough and the Stars" the characters seem to me part of their environment; and though the construction is of the loosest, the development, if not perhaps inevitable, is logical.

SMILES AND TEARS

Mr. O'Casey does not deal in heroes or heroines. His real concern, as I see it, is with individuals as members of a group, and it is the skill with which he translates into dramatic form the interplay of the emotions inside the group that makes him unique amongst Irish dramatists. We get this in comedy in the two opening Acts which contain more laughs than anything the author has yet given us, though dramatically it would probably improve the play were they compressed into one.

Yet I should hate to see sacrificed Uncle Peter at the tea-table arrayed in all the glory of his Forester's uniform with the Citizen Army mobilising in the street, or the heroic encounter as a result of too many "balls of malt" between

Bessie Burgess and Mrs. Gogan in the corner public-house. And if the opening Acts were fused there are other episodes equally good that would have to go.

In this play, unlike "Juno," the tragic note is sounded only in the last Act. But there is no mistake about the vigor with which Mr. O'Casey sounds it. He makes more vivid than any of our dramatists before him the brutal crash of war and bloodshed upon the lives of ordinary people.

NO POLEMICS

There is no hint of polemics, no question of taking sides. It is not a question of whether Commandant Clitheroe, of the Citizen Army, is right, or Bessie Burgess, who chants "Rule Britannia" wrong. What the play drives home is the strength of the common ties that bind humanity, the impulse that nerves the virago Bessie to face a storm of bullets to bring aid to a sick woman, and raises drunken Fluther Good almost to heroic level.

I am convinced Mr. O'Casey would be even more effective if he did not heap up the corpses so lavishly. The last Act has Elizabethan precedents in its favour, but that is the best that can be said for it.

SPLENDID ACTING

The acting was as good as I have seen at the Abbey. There was a fear that the absence of Miss Allgood would make a difference, but Miss Maureen Delany, in her part as Bessie Burgess, made one of the big hits of the play. She has never lacked forcefulness, but last night she combined it with restraint, and her tragic passages were finely handled. Miss May Craig painted an unforgettable portrait of the depressing Mrs. Gogan, whose talk is all of graves and epitaphs; and Miss Ria Mooney, as Rosie Redmond, managed a difficult part admirably.

If the play has a heroine, it is Nora. Unfortunately, she is not an altogether convincing figure, though the fault rests with the dramatist, and not with Miss Shelah Richards, who was excellent in the first Act, and did make something of the last scene, though a mad woman in a nightgown is always too reminiscent of Hamlet burlesque.

One does not need to praise Mr. Barry Fitzgerald. It is sufficient to say his Fluther Good is in his best style. He is splendidly partnered by Eric Gorman and Michael J. Dolan.

J. W. C. [2]

As usual, Joseph Holloway was there, and his journal entry indicated that he was as much interested in the "Dublin Set" as in the play. Holloway's comments are valuable because they exhibit a cautionary note that not everyone was as enthused as the critics.

Monday, February 8. There was electricity in the air before and behind the curtain at the Abbey to-night when Sean O'Casey's play *The Plough and the Stars* was first produced. The theatre was thronged with distinguished people, and before the doors opened the queue to the pit entrance extended past old Abbey Street—not a quarter of them got in. The play was followed with feverish interest, and the players being called and recalled at the end of the piece. Loud calls for "Author!" brought O'Casey on the stage and he received an ovation.

Monty [?] said after Act II, "I am glad I am off duty." Some of the incidents in Acts I and II had proved too much for the Censor in him. Mr. Reddin, after Act III said, "The play leaves a bad taste in the mouth." George O'Brien was happy after Act II when he saw it went without any opposition. . . . The dialogue at times seemed too long and wordy, kept back the action, and will have to be tightened up. . . . The second act carries realism to extremes. On the whole, it falls far short of *Juno and the Paycock*.

F. R. Higgins,* Liam O'Flaherty* and others were in a group. Ernest Blythe* and Mrs., the Lord Chief Justice and Mrs. Kennedy, Kevin Higgins, Yeats and party steered into the Greenroom after Act II. [Lennox] Robinson was about also. T. C. Murray* . . . Andrew [E.] Malone* . . . F[rank] H[ugh] O'Donnell.* Sean O'Casey contented himself with standing room on the balcony. . . . I wished O'Casey luck before the piece. The first-night audience stamped the play with their approval in no uncertain way. . . .

The street outside the theatre was packed on either side with motor cars. In Abbey Street a policeman was stalking after four "Rosie Redmonds" [prostitutes] who flew before him, and I am sure the dispersing audience found no interest in their flight, although they had applauded "Rosie" plying her trade in Act II of *The Plough and the Stars*. The fight between the two women in the pub scene was longly applauded, yet who is not disgusted with such an exhibition when one chances on it in real life?[3]

The second night witnessed another full house, but this time there were warnings of the explosion to come, now only two nights away. Holloway wrote:

> Tuesday, February 9. The Abbey was again thronged. I saw . . . Sean O'Casey whom I congratulated on last night's success (the receipts are heaping up steadily in London for *Juno*—fell twopence last week). . . . Some four or five in the pit objected to the [Irish] Volunteers bringing the flag into a pub in Act II. Kevin Barry's sister was one of the objectors. The pit door had to be shut to avoid a rush being made on it, and two policemen were on the scene. The audience relished the fight of the women in Act II and didn't object to the nasty incidents and phrases scattered here and there throughout the play. . . . Lord Chief Justice Kennedy declared he thought it was abominable. Kevin Higgins was silent until Monty thanked God he was off duty [again!], and added, "This is a lovely Irish export." Then O'Higgins owned up he didn't like it. Meeting Dr. Oliver Gogarty,* Monty said, "I hope you are not going to say you liked it?"
>
> "I do," owned up Gogarty (whose reputation for filthy limericks is very widespread). "It'll give the smugminded something to think about."[4]

The following day, O'Casey wrote to Sara Allgood in London. *Juno* was doing as well as the *Plough*, and congratulations were in order for everybody. In the letter, O'Casey gave his impressions of the Abbey company, for whom he had great respect but also with whom he had had trouble. The importance of this letter may be in the last paragraph, for in the ensuing weeks O'Casey continued to complain about his eyes. Later, the illness (glaucoma) would become a major factor.

Dublin
10 February 1926

My dear Sally,

Ah, thanks indeed to you for your very kind telegram wishing me success, & thanks again & more than thanks for your message to [Maureen] Delany.

You'll never be able, Sally, to close up your warm & generous heart.

The play went splendidly, & the bookings have broken all records. Maureen was really very good, & worked like a Trojan woman.

We had a little trouble when the play was being cast, Miss Crowe objecting to a good deal of the dialogue in her part (grand dialogue too) & May Craig had to take her place.

Shelia Richards was, I think, magnificent in the part of young Nora: she has, I believe, in her something of the genius of Sally Allgood—that's saying a hell of a lot!

I have heard you have had a bad cold, I hope you are all right by now.

My own eyes are troubling me, and the surgeon has ordered no writing or reading for a little time, so I have to be as brief as possible, but I couldn't stay easy from sending you my best thanks.

Yours,
Sean[5]

The third night was again sold out and O'Casey was still the toast of Dublin. However, there were more signs of trouble, and, if Holloway's observations are correct, the strain was beginning to show on the Abbey actors.

Wednesday, February 10. At the Abbey, I saw Frank Hugh O'Donnell on the balcony during Act II. He joined Sean O'Casey and a lady in the vestibule . . . O'Casey was besieged by young ladies on the balcony to sign his autograph in their programmes, and on a gentleman asking him to do so for him, O'Casey replied, "I only do so for young and pretty girls." . . .

A sort of moaning was to be heard to-night from the pit during the "Rosie Redmond" episode and when the

Volunteers brought in the flags to the pub. (I noticed Arthur Shields unfurled his tricolour, as he came in, in a defiant manner. He usually is out for cheap notoriety, such as repeating dirty remarks in *The Playboy*, usually omitted in representation). . . . The actors rattle through those interminable word-twisters in a gabby, inflectionless manner. Miss Delany repeats much she has to say in a loud, monotonous, meaningless way, and Barry Fitzgerald fails to articulate clearly in his longer speeches. When he is silent, he is usually drollish; witness his facial expression when asked to take the baby in Act II![6]

On Thursday, 11 February 1926, the Abbey exploded. During Act II, the audience began to hiss, boo, and heckle, drowning out much of the dialogue. By Act III there was pandemonium. A *Manchester Guardian* article described the action and Yeats's famous speech.

Twenty women rushed from the pit to the stalls. Two of them succeeded in reaching the stage, where a general melee took place. The invading women were thrown bodily back into the orchestra. A young man then tried to reach the stage, but was cut off by the lowering of the curtain. This he grabbed, swinging out on it in a frantic endeavour to pull it down. Women rushed to aid him in his project, but he was suddenly thrown into the stalls by a sharp blow from one of the actors. The pandemonium created a panic among a section of the audience, who dashed for the exits and added to the confusion.

As soon as the curtain was raised again, up dashed another youth to the stage and got into grips with two actresses opening the next scene. Immediately a couple of actors rushed from the wings and unceremoniously pushed off the intruder. Another man had got on the stage by this time and was attacked by a number of players. He retaliated vigorously, and after several blows were exchanged, a hardy punch on the jaw [by Barry Fitzgerald] hurled him into the stalls.

Meanwhile altercations were going on among the two sections of the audience. For several minutes the players calmly walked up and down the stage, but the performance was not resumed. A change came over the troubled scene when a party of detectives and uniformed police arrived and quickly distributed themselves through different parts of the house.

Senator W. B. Yeats, the well-known poet and dramatist, who is a director of the theatre, came forward to the accompaniment of a torrent of boos and hisses. What he said was quite inaudible to a large section of the audience who knew he was speaking only by the movement of his lips and the waving of his hands in dramatic gesture. This was his speech: "I thought you had got tired of this. It commenced fifteen years ago. You have disgraced yourselves again. Is this to be an ever-recurring celebration of the arrival of Irish genius? Once more you have rocked the cradle of genius. The news of this will go from country to country. You have once more rocked the cradle of a reputation. The fame of O'Casey is born tonight. This is his apotheosis."

As Senator Yeats retired, shouts of "We want the play," mingled with cries of "Up the Republic!" Over a dozen women demonstrators seized a number of front row seats, vacated by people who had rushed away in panic. The women began to sing the "Soldier's Song" [the Irish national anthem], and the chorus was quickly taken up in the gallery. Three or four police approached the women and ejected a number of them, while others fled to the pit.

The removal of these demonstrators marked the beginning of the defeat of the disturbers. Mrs. [Hannah] Sheehy-Skeffington* rose and announced that "we are now leaving the hall under police protection. I am," she added, "one of the widows of Easter Week. It is no wonder that you do not remember the men of Easter Week because none of you fought on either side. The play is going to London soon to be advertised there because it belies Ireland. All you need do now is to sing 'God Save the King.' " She then left.[7]

The only other objective coverage of the disturbances was printed in the *Irish Times* which had its own reporter present at the theatre. Historians will note that this version of Yeats's famous speech is at variance with that reported by the *Manchester Guardian.* Perhaps no one will ever know exactly what Yeats said, though there is little argument about the substance of the speech.

ABBEY THEATRE SCENE
AN ATTEMPT TO STOP MR. O'CASEY'S NEW PLAY
FIGHT ON STAGE
ACTRESSES STRUCK BY MAN FROM AUDIENCE
WOMEN EJECTED

Mr. Sean O'Casey's new play, "The Plough and the Stars," was the cause of scenes in the Abbey Theatre, Dublin, last night reminiscent of the days, close on twenty years ago, when a prolonged and organised, but unsuccessful, effort was made to prevent the showing of Synge's "Playboy of the Western World."

"The Plough and the Stars" presents a picture of tenement life in Dublin before and during the Easter Week rebellion, 1916, and the four acts show the reactions of that event on the lives of the poorest in the city.

At the first performance on Monday night the play and its author had an enthusiastic reception. On Tuesday night there was a scene in the back pit, when six women sitting together tried by voice and foot to prevent the hearing of the concluding part of the second act, in which the happenings in a public-house in tenement land are depicted. The interruption lasted only a minute or two. On Wednesday night one woman made a very feeble demonstration.

Last night, the situation assumed a more serious aspect. From the start of the play there were minor incidents, such as stamping of feet, hissing and shouting. Those came mostly from the pit. When the curtain went up for the second act there began a pandemonium which continued until the curtain fell. It was carried on for the most part by women, who shouted, boohed and sang, occasionally varying their demonstration by a set speech.

The noise was intensified by counter-demonstrations of applause by the majority of the audience. The players carried on in dumb show, and in the second act hardly a word of the dialogue was heard. In their unflinching stubbornness the company followed the example of their predecessors of the "Playboy" days.

THE INTERRUPTERS

When the lights went up at the end of the second act everyone could see many women who are prominently identified with Republican demonstrations in the city. Shocking epithets were hurled at Miss Ria Mooney while she played Rosie Redmond in pantomime, but the wrath of the interrupters was for the most part directed against the political significance of the play, its brutal exposition of what took place in the homes of the rank and file of the Citizen Army, while the leaders were making speeches about freedom in the abstract.

FIGHT ON THE STAGE

After the start of the third act, notable for Mrs. Clitheroe's description of what she saw of the fighting in the streets, when, half demented, she sought her husband, about a dozen women made their way from the pit on either side of the theatre and attempted to scramble on to the stage. After a time they succeeded, and there ensued on the stage a regular fight between the players and the invaders.

One young man succeeded in getting on to the stage along with the women. He deliberately struck Miss Maureen Delany in the face, and then aimed a blow at Miss May Craig. In a moment Mr. Barry Fitzgerald ("Fluther Good") with one blow sent him sprawling to the wings.

The play, of course, was stopped, and the curtain was lowered. The women demonstrators were bundled off the stage by the male members of the company and the attendants. In a high state of hysteria they were pushed out of the theatre altogether.

It was difficult to see how it was done, but the stage appeared to be cleared in very quick time, and Senator W. B.

Yeats, one of the directors of the theatre, came forward to address the audience.

SPEECH BY SENATOR YEATS

During the few minutes that those incidents occupied, a number of people, probably thinking that the final curtain for the night had been rung down, left their seats in the stalls to go home. A number of women swarmed from the pit into the empty chairs and kept up a din while Dr. Yeats was speaking.

In a lull, here and there, he was heard to say that once again a minority in Dublin had tried to disgrace the reputation of the city.

"Is this," he shouted, "going to be a recurring celebration of Irish genius? Synge first, and then O'Casey! The news of the happenings of the last few minutes here will flash from country to country. Dublin has once more rocked the cradle of a reputation. From such a scene in this theatre went forth the fame of Synge. Equally the fame of O'Casey is born here tonight. This is his apotheosis."

DETECTIVES ARRIVE

Suddenly and unexpectedly the shrieks and turmoil from the pit and from the invaded stalls died down, almost before Dr. Yeats had finished. The explanation was found with the arrival of half-a-dozen men of the detective branch, who had heard unofficially that an attempt was on foot to wreck the theatre. They took up positions here and there, in the noisiest centers on the floor of the house, and the noise ceased almost entirely.

The next unexpected incident was the raising of the curtain and the continuance of the interrupted Act 3. This was hailed with a wild burst of enthusiasm from the general body of the audience, in which the counter-demonstration was entirely drowned. The members of the company on at the time proceeded to take up the thread of the act as if nothing had happened. They finished the fourth act, and finished the play, and the audience left scarcely five minutes later than the usual time.

WOMEN EJECTED

After the resumption of the play half-a-dozen women, who had taken possession of the front row of the stalls, kept up a fire of interruption, until they were forcibly ejected from the theatre by the uniformed policemen, who had been summoned. One of the women protested against her removal as an interference with personal liberty. Another woman, in a high staccato voice, made a speech from the balcony until she was invited to go out, and took the advice.

From start to finish the whole thing was a woman's row, made and carried on by women. It is, perhaps, significant, under the circumstances, that Mr. O'Casey's play is directed mainly to show to the world the misery of the lives of the women population of the tenement rooms of Dublin.

The net result was that little damage was done, except perhaps to the face of the man that Barry Fitzgerald tackled on stage. Two of the footlight lamps were injured, and portions of the curtain were torn. The orchestra lost a few sheets of music (which were torn) and the cover of Mr. Fred Deane's double bass fiddle. There was no necessity for arrests as in the "Playboy" scenes.

PLAYERS THANKED

The most remarkable incident of the whole evening happened after everyone had left and the doors of the theatre were closed. It took place in the green room, when the whole company of the players—men and women, some with the grease paint but half off their faces—gathered around Dr. Yeats to assure him of their determination to carry on.

Addressing them, he expressed his admiration of their conduct that evening. He said that they and their theatre had got an advertisement of the utmost value in the eyes of the whole world. Such an incident could not take place in the commercial theatre. That such a small minority could be found in Dublin to try to stop the showing of Mr. O'Casey's play was a proof to him that Mr. O'Casey had in "The Plough and the Stars" cut very close to the bone.

RUN MAY BE EXTENDED

An Irish Times reporter was informed that last night's display will not in any way interfere with the continuance of the play in its entirety. Furthermore, the directors will take into serious consideration the suggestion from many members of the audience that it should be put on again next week. The intention was to finish the initial run of "The Plough and the Stars" to-morrow night and to put on "Doctor Knock" from Tuesday of next week. The number of people who have been unable to book this week is sufficiently large enough to fill the house for another seven performances.

Simple effective steps have been taken to ensure, first, the safety from molestation of the theatre and all connected with it, and secondly, the comfort of each succeeding audience. There can, we are assured, be no repetition of last night's attempt to prevent theatre-goers from seeing Mr. O'Casey's remarkable play.[8]

Everybody at the theatre that night saw something different. The following three eyewitness accounts, two of which were published in major newspapers the next day, demonstrate the fallibility of such accounts and also the contradictory evidence historians would later have to sift through. The first account is by Joseph Holloway, who was again present to record in his journal who did what to whom.

Thursday, February 11. The protest of Tuesday night having no effect on the management, a great protest was made to-night, and ended in almost the second act being played in dumb show, and pantomiming afterwards. People spoke from all parts of the house, and W. B. Yeats moved out from the stalls during the noise, and Kathleen O'Brennan, who came in afterwards, told me Yeats went round to *The Irish Times* office to try to have the report of the row doctored. On his return to the theatre, he tried to get a hearing on the stage, but not a word he spoke could be heard. Nulty was in great *Irish Times* form, foaming against those who objected to the play, and vowing he'd write up Dorothy

Macardle,* who was one of the protestors to the Volunteers' introduction into the pub on Tuesday last, and accuse her of doing so because of the failure of her play, *Ann Kavanagh*. I reminded him that that would be an untruth, as the play has always been well received and liked.

I am sorry to say that I was incorrect in my judgement as to what Abbey audiences could stand when I told George O'Brien on Monday before Act II that they would stand even the devils in Hell exhibiting their worst pranks in silence sooner than make another objectionable play like *The Playboy* burst into notoriety by their disapproval. But, alas, to-night's protest has made a second *Playboy* of *The Plough and the Stars*, and Yeats was in his element at last. . . .

After Act I was the first I heard that a storm was brewing from Dan Breen,* who was speaking to Kavanagh and said, "Mrs. Pearse, Mrs. Tom Clarke, Mrs. Sheehy-Skeffington, and others were in the theatre to vindicate the manhood of 1916." . . .

Few really like the play as it stands, and most who saw it are in sympathy with those who protested. Some of the players behaved with uncommon roughness to some ladies who got on to the stage, and threw two of them into the stalls. One young man thrown from the stage got his side hurt by the piano. The chairs of the orchestra were thrown on the stage, and the music on the piano fluttered, and some four or five tried to pull down half of the drop curtain, and another caught hold of one side of the railing in the scene in Act III.

The players headed by [F. J.] McCormick as spokesman lined up onstage, and Mac tried to make himself heard without avail. Then a man came on and begged the audience to give the actor a hearing, and they did, and Mac said he wished the actors should be treated distinct from the play, etc., and his speech met with applause. Then the play proceeded in fits and starts to the end, and the whole house in a state of excitement.

Mrs. Fay protested to me that the play didn't get a hearing. Mrs. Sheehy-Skeffington from the back of the balcony during the din kept holding forth, and at the same time others were speaking in the pit; all were connected with Easter Week. A great big voice called, "O'Casey Out!" on "Rosie Redmond" appearing in Act II. Shouts of "Honor Bright" were heard.⁹

Others also heard the cry of "Honor Bright," a reference to a recently murdered Dublin prostitute. It was not clear, though, whether or not the protesters wanted Rosie Redmond to meet the same fate.

Stephen Gwynn,* one of Ireland's most respected journalists and writing for the London *Observer*, did not attend the production and relied on an eyewitness report from a "friend"—an odd way to do dramatic criticism.

> Mr. O'Casey's play has made a sensation in Dublin. It was produced on Monday, and proved to be a fresh exposition of his view that humanity is more than nationality and that warfare is an inhuman thing, even when nationality is its plea. But this time he illustrates from Easter Week of 1916, which was the heroic period of the Irish insurrectionary movement; and he shows in dramatic chronicle what that heroic struggle meant in flesh and blood to the masses of Dublin.
>
> Some resentment apparently was shown on the first night; on Tuesday there was a small demonstration of hostility; on Wednesday it increased; and on Thursday the stage was rushed by a crowd, mostly of women—who are said to have been Republicans. The play was stopped for a while, but on the arrival of plain-clothes police quiet returned and the last acts were finished.
>
> At the end of it, the actors crowded round Senator Yeats, chief director of the theatre, and told him that they were determined to carry on. Mr. Yeats came in front and made a fierce speech, telling the audience in effect that they had disgraced Ireland.
>
> I have not myself been able to be in Dublin, but a friend sends me an account of what happened on Thursday night:
>
> "Back from a very rowdy evening, having heard with difficulty two acts (first and last of the four that there are), and much of a Republican demonstration, curiously illogical, headed by Mrs. Sheehy-Skeffington, and also a threat that the Abbey might be blown up, as the cinema was, on the

charge of Free State propaganda. Where that came in, I could not say; but about twenty ardent young women and a few young men did their best to pull the curtains down, swinging from them and kicking over footlights.

"Act II opens in a public-house with a young 'Honor Bright' (this is the name of a Dublin street-walker who was recently the victim in a horrible murder case) standing bewailing that there will be nothing doing, for they all have faces of saints while marching. Meantime the meeting goes on outside.

"At this, there came from the audience shouts of 'Honor Bright' and boos and cries for O'Casey to appear; and then Mrs. Skeffy got up and orated and said this act should be cut and that it was traducing the men of 1916 and would be sent as such to England, etc. etc.; and, to judge from the noise, she must have had a quarter of the audience with her. Meantime, the play went on in dumb show: I could not hear a word save Mrs. S. Yeats left his seat hurriedly.

"Act III: The consumptive child and May Craig, the mother, in the street outside the house. At this there were screams of 'Pull down the curtain,' and so much row that in three minutes, when four or five of the hardy young females leapt from the audience on the stage and swung on it, it did fall. They swarmed then and tore a good deal and knocked the footlights over, and we all were, I think, a little uneasy about fire. Then all the actors—about twenty or thirty—appeared, really angry, all gesticulating and trying to get leave to speak.

"Scuffles, wordy and otherwise, went on in all corners of the audience, and Mrs. S. continued to orate.

"Then the curtain went up on a stiff, pompous, and furious Yeats, and he was yelled at and quite inaudible, save that I heard, 'This will go all over the world.' But I was glad he appeared; only it ought to have been sooner, for at that moment the police poured in and began taking out the women. More hubbub; and finally Dolan said they would begin again; and for the third time the curtain rose. The rest of the act, a short scene—firing, a volunteer carried in wounded—was mostly dumb show, but they finished it.

"Act IV—House now about half full. Maureen Delany, as

the wife of the Dublin Fusiler, and Mrs. Commandant, who has gone off her head and wanders about in her nightdress—wonderful acting. Four men playing cards—a raid by Tommies—Maureen D. shot at the window—and a man comes in to say the Commandant is killed; again most poignant tragedy and the kind of thing O'Casey does really well. From the audience very little noise, as most of the disturbers had been cleared and Mrs. S. had departed, saying she left us to our police protection.

"For the life of me I could see no British or Free State propaganda; only a very realistic and dramatic first and last act; much washing of our dirty linen in public (about which I rather agree with the lady); most despicable men, and wonderfully moving and fine women. I take it O'Casey is a rather disillusioned fellow about heroes and the like, and he knew quite well it was the dwellers in the tenements who got it always in the neck. I should say the first and last acts were the best of O'Casey's I've seen; no wearisome speeches, and there seemed all through more cohesion.

"Yeats, alas, was just furious (I don't blame him) and waited too long to appear. I think the introduction of the 'Honor Bright' (when it is fresh in everyone's mind, and a case not handled to our credit) has a good deal to say to the row."[10]

The *Evening Herald's* account was also from an eyewitness, though this writer was clearly confused about the reason for the protest and seemed to be upset because he didn't get his money's worth. Some might say he got more than his money's worth.

NEW PLAY RESENTED

LAST NIGHT'S SCENES IN THE ABBEY THEATRE

1916 MEMORIES

ONLOOKER'S IMPRESSIONS OF PEOPLE'S PROTEST

The article below is specially contributed to the "Evening Herald" by one who witnessed the demonstration against the "Plough and the Stars," Mr. Sean O'Casey's new play, in the Abbey Theatre last night.

It is very depressing to go to the theatre, pay for one's seat, and hear nothing of the play, and I wondered if the box office would consider that the people had a grievance, as well as Senator Yeats, and return the money for the seats which they had to vacate.

This was my chief grievance until I saw Senator Yeats on the stage of the Abbey Theatre last night in a Sydney Carton attitude, correct pose; arms raised in studied movement, to make a characteristic speech, and having failed to get his voice overheard he hurled epithets at the audience which refused to listen. I also began to think. Evidently Senator Yeats has made up his mind that the plain people of Dublin have no right to think—but I made that mistake.

EXCITED CROWD

I looked around and saw one of the most excited crowds that ever assembled in the theatre. It was not an organised mob. The gallery and pit were the same as usual, supported by the people. I did not know that Mr. O'Casey's new play had caused any protest during the week. Indeed, the reports of the play, with the exception of the "Herald" critique, gave no indication that it contained anything objectionable. Therefore, when the second act was put on and a group of women rushed the stage and tried to prevent the performance, I tried to understand what was the reason. When the din began and the stalls, as usual, quickly emptied, I tried to gather from all around why the people were so infuriated.

That the tactics adopted by the women were bad is certain. They have advertised a play that would probably have given as much offence to the stalls as to the plain people, but Irish blood is hot and the feeling last night in the theatre was desperate.

THE MORAL STANDARD

Nevertheless, feeling does not run high without a reason, and it showed to those who are in doubt that people are not "half alive" when it comes to something fundamentally affecting the Irish race, and this, in spite of recent happenings, unfortunate to the reputation of our city, is the moral standard of the Irish people.

It would appear the second Act is the objectionable part in Mr. O'Casey's play. It is objectionable to a large section of the people. It is repulsive for several reasons, and such a play would not be permitted by the Government of any other country—certainly not in America, France, Germany, or under Mussolini at the present time. So that Senator Yeats, who is as well a leader of the Art movement, but also a politician, and a representative of the people, ought to know this. There is an effort abroad to destroy nationalism and supplant it by internationalism, and the desecration of the National flag of a country. I should imagine the play would come under the Treason Act. It is quite possible that during the world war national flags were carried into the publichouses, and it is evident that Mr. O'Casey saw such an incident. But what are national censors for? There was an effort, too, last night to turn the incident into a political split, but this did not succeed. Free Staters and Republicans seemed to resent what they considered an attempt to desecrate the Easter Week rising and the memory of the dead.

PEARSE'S SPEECH

I understand that the speech of Padraic Pearse is the one used by Mr. O'Casey in his play, and the world as well as Ireland knows the character of the leaders of the Easter Week Rising. It was a well-known fact that they were pioneers in the temperance movement. It is absurd to imagine or state the Volunteers were teetotallers, but what those who hold Easter Week sacred feel is that while the Abbey Theatre is quite willing to minimise the sacrifice of the men who went out and the sufferings of their relatives, no other nation would permit this insult to the nation which permeates the second act.

AN IRISH EPIC

Mr. O'Casey is writing of things as he knows them; so could others. Has Senator Yeats yet had the courage to produce a play dealing with Easter Week—of the poets who threw aside the laurels, the visionaries and dreamers who forsook the flowered path of literary reward for their country? Yet Easter Week has inspired the idealists of the world. The magnificent gesture of the poets and artists who went to death for love of their people, with no fanfare of trumpets, in Easter Week, was one of the greatest epics of history. Let us have both sides in the Abbey Theatre, and there will be some tolerance in Dublin. It is all very well to show courage in producing plays and talk tolerance when but one point of view is shown, and that the minority. Let us have both.

A French critic wrote that to a large extent French drama was written for export, and that the great output was exported to advantage. For years the French people, whom Senator Yeats so valiantly defended in the Senate recently, were represented abroad by these plays, and in consequence a French social life to suit the foreigner had to be created. In fact, the French life as shown to the tourist is not real France.

It would appear that some of our dramatists are writing for export, but is there not a danger also, too, that we may by such plays bring to our cities a class of such undesirables that may menace the very life of our nationhood and take a generation to destroy?

We are not provincial people, and, although I had to vacate my seat at the theatre last night, yet I feel glad that there is vitality enough in Dublin to make a protest against this one-sided view of Irish life, which is not playing fair to the Irish race.[11]

It is evident from the reviews that the Abbey players were excellent. They were so good, in fact, that when Yeats wrote to H. J. C. Grierson shortly after, he commented:

You may have noticed that we have had riots in the theatre again. I was with you when word reached me of the Playboy row. This time we had a packed theatre every day while the play was running, indeed numbers could not get in. The riot was soon over and displayed one curious effect of fine acting. When the Republicans rushed the stage a man caught up a girl [Kitty Curling], who had been playing a consumptive invalid, and folded her in a cloak as a preliminary to carrying her from the stage—she was not the actress in his eyes but a consumptive girl.[12]

The Friday night performance was quiet and subdued. The theatre was filled with detectives and things were so boring that Holloway left at the end of Act II.

On Saturday the weekly papers appeared. Walter Starkie* wrote an incisive review of the play for the *Irish Statesman*, and the *Voice of Labour*, journal of the Irish trade union movement, indicted O'Casey for his treatment of Irish nationalism. Both papers were caught unawares by the disturbances two nights previous and neither mentioned them in the reviews, which had obviously been written before Thursday. Of particular interest was an editorial by the *Irish Times* which used the protests as an excuse for a scathing attack on the educational system and for rebuffing demands for censorship.

CANT AND FACTS

Has education made any progess in Southern Ireland during the last thirty years? This humiliating question is suggested by the tumult, on Thursday evening, at the Abbey Theatre. The fruits of education—even of a sound elementary education—are intellectual dignity, tolerance, a sense of proportion, readiness to hear arguments and to consider new ideas on their merits. In spite of the vast sums which British and Irish Governments have spent on education in our country since 1900, there are, in this year of Grace, numbers of Irishmen and Irishwomen whose only answers to arguments that displease them are the raucous shout and the closed fist. Nearly a generation ago, "The Countess Cathleen" was howled down in Dublin because it dealt in allegory with a profound problem of religious sacrifice. In 1907 "The Playboy of the Western World" received like treatment because it was a satire on certain failings of the Irish peasant's character. This week, "The Plough and the Stars" is condemned, and its actors are assaulted, because it throws on a phase of Irish politics the gleam of a true artist's insight and sympathy. The interruptors of Thursday night's performance imagined, in Mr. O'Casey's picture of the reactions of the Easter Rebellion on the Dublin slums, an insult to the memory of Patrick Pearse; and their retort was not an argument, but a paroxysm. Religion, national character, politics—these three things are in all civilised lands the very stuff of literature. If they must be banished from Irish letters, and banished through no play of reason, but by brute force, can we claim that Ireland is a civilised land?

Since intolerance springs from refusal to see what one does not wish to see, it is found usually in close company with cant. Cant is that comfortable attitude which cultivates the sensation of virtue at the expense of fact. It seems that the objections to Mr. O'Casey's play are not wholly political. He is the Hogarth of Dublin tenements; he shrinks from no aspect of their humanity, and he brings a street-walker into "The Plough and the Stars." This audacity has shocked some citizens of Dublin. How far, they say, is the licence of the theatre to venture? Is it not terrible that the young should run the risk of seeing a mimic street-walker behind the footlights? Will not the Government make haste to introduce a dramatic censorship? Such talk makes us anxious to exchange all the literary talent now rampant in this country for one Irish Juvenal. The young citizens of Dublin need not pay anything to see counterfeit prostitution on the stage of the Abbey Theatre. They can rub shoulders with the real thing on every night of the week in the central streets. There are few other cities in these islands where youth is more oblivious to the moral and physical dangers of sexual vice; and there is none where the temptations to excessive drinking are more frequent and more flagrant. Yet we have no fierce agitation against these things: public opinion and its guides conspire to ignore them. It is only when a prophet like Mr. O'Casey traces the malady to its source and paints the conditions which create street-walkers, that the name of decency is invoked to hide the unpalatable truth.

We detect the smug voice of cant also in the demand for a moral censorship of the Press. Some people have asked the Free State government to prohibit the importation of indecent books and newspapers—especially Sunday newspapers— from England. The Minister for Justice, as we are glad to see, is moving cautiously in the matter. He has asked five persons to consider whether it is "necessary or ad-

> visable, in the interests of public morality, to extend the existing power of the State to prohibit or restrict the sale and circulation of printed matter." It will be noted that these terms of reference do not exclude matter printed in the *Saorstat;* and we should welcome their scope if we believed that a moral censorship of the Press would have any good results. We hold, however, that such a censorship merely would feed the national vice of self-complacency and would divert public attention from more urgent perils. The things that defile Ireland to-day come not from without, but from within. If the vulgar and indecent contents of a few English newspapers have power to warp Irish brains and to damn Irish souls, we are brought back to the point from which we started. Parents, schools, and Churches—not English newspapers—must bear the blame if young Irishmen and Irishwomen are sent into the business of life without the carapace of character and the archangel's spear of taste and intellectual discrimination. Our people's first need today is to clear their minds of cant. We are not better than all other nations—we are worse than some of them. Our educational system, judged by results, is lamentable. Our own institutions—our filthy tenements and myriad drink-shops—breed the vices which will continue to sap the nation's strength until we choose to see ourselves as we are.[13]

Walter Starkie's review for the *Irish Statesman* was a model of sympathy and encouragement, and he presented one of the few dramatic critiques untainted by emotionalism.

THE PLOUGH AND THE STARS

> When gazing at the audience stacked in every corner of the Abbey Theatre last Monday night, it was impossible not to feel how direct is the influence exercised by the Abbey Theatre over Dublin life. And then we thought of three moments of the theatre in its evolution. At first it was poetry when poets dreamt in their ivory tower of far off legends heard faintly down the centuries. Then appeared "Countess

Cathleen" and other plays. The stage had rediscovered poetry as its natural expression. Then descended the passionate temperament of Synge and made the Western folk speak in drama which gives the nourishment on which our imagination lives. Then followed the long list of playwrights who drew their inspiration from rustic scenes. Gradually the stage drama became more and more influenced by modern problems and became psychological in tendency. Now, in Sean O'Casey, there is the city drama as opposed to the traditional country drama, and it is no varnished tableau that he shows us, but the bitter, crude reality which he has observed in his walks through the streets. But Sean O'Casey is not a social dramatist like most of the moderns, filled with a desire to expose some vice and correct by developing one thesis in his play. He looks at our society from all sides and his fund of sympathy is large enough to include all. But though he pardons all, he never fails to expose hypocrisies and evil to the gaze of humanity. No dramatist is more characteristic if we want to show the difference between the English and the Irish artist. Sean O'Casey is not English or Teuton; he is Mediterranean. For a Mediterranean the most important thing is not the essence of a thing, but its presence, its actuality. What Emerson says of Goethe might be applied to Mr. O'Casey: "he sees at every pore." In his latest play he paints on a large canvas his impression of the 1916 Rebellion. In the first two acts we see the preparations made, we watch the development of the tragedy: in the last two acts we watch its consummation. The whole edifice of the old society crumbles amid the flames which light up the sky as if Walhalla were burning. But amid all the slaughter and fire, is there hope and glorious promise? Mr. O'Casey does not show us the flicker; he leaves us at the end before the darkened stage with nothing but misery in our hearts. "Oh, the senselessness of it all!" What can humanity over the whole world obtain by torturing itself on the rack of war? Let the war be in Ireland or in France or in Russia, it is all the same senseless war dictated by narrow nationalist ideas, and we remember the Covey's words: "There's no such thing as an Irishman or an Englishman, or a German, or a Turk; we're all only human bein's." The last act of "The Plough and the Stars" is the biggest thing that Mr. O'Casey has done yet: it is so sincere, so direct, so purged of rhetoric and sentimentality, that it reaches the level of great tragedy. And it rises up to tragedy on account of its human appeal. The slightest extra touch and it would become Adelphi melodrama. There is hardly another dramatist who could work up that scene between the mad woman and Mrs. Burgess without making it grotesquely hideous. But Mr. O'Casey held his audience spellbound and produced on them the true Aristotelian catharsis. Let us visualise the scene: the coffin laid across two chairs, two candles lit near by: the windows red with the glare from the burning city: the four men silently playing cards on the floor. And in the corner, terrified, stands the poor mad Nora. In Act II, the fight between the two men gave too symmetrical an impression to the scene: it resembled the knockabout of the old Harlequinade. In fact, our impression at the first performance was that much of the business in Act II and Act III could be shortened. The acting of Miss Ria Mooney as Rosie, the daughter of the "digs," was so remarkable that it held the public.

Each act of the play gives a complete picture of slum life, and Mr. O'Casey is as simple and direct in his methods as [Henri Francois] Becque [the French dramatist] with his *tranches de vie.*

The first act introduces us to the Clitheroe family. Jack and Nora are newly married and still have some illusions left. Then there is the cousin called The Covey, who is a Socialist and hopes for a war which will emancipate the proletariat; and Peter Flynn, a fretful little man always at war with everybody, but anxious to display his dignity as a member of the Foresters. But above all there is Fluther Good: he is a man of forty years of age who early surrenders to thoughts of anxiety, fond of his "oil," but determined to conquer the habit before he dies. At once we recognise in him a successor to Joxer. One of Mr. O'Casey's mannerisms is to label his characters with special set words or phrases which accompany them through the play. They perform an analogous function to the "Leit Motivs" in music. We remember Joxer's phrase, "Oh! he's a darlin' man, a daarlin' man." Fluther uses the word "derogatory" on every occasion possible. Fluther is the central character of the play; he is as important to its structure as Harlequin or Brighella used to be to the ancient *commedia dell'arte*. He has a philosophy of his own which permits him to make the best of everything. He can dispute over religion with the Covey, he can walk out with Rosie, he can loot a jar of whiskey and become as frenzied and Bacchanalian as Nannie, he can risk his life amid bullets to try and help the distressed womenfolk. He is the complete man of the world, and Sean O'Casey created him lovingly. He lives for us more than Joxer or Seumas Shields. The interpretation of his personality given by Mr. Barry Fitzgerald was one of the best pieces of acting I have seen lately at the Abbey. A great deal of the humour of the play falls to Fluther's share, for Mr. O'Casey always has him at hand to relieve the tragic situation by his humorous comment. And it is only when he has been led off by the Tommies in the last act that the tragedy descends like a black pall. Mrs. Bessie Burgess, who might be called the heroine of the tragedy, as she is the victim, has all the vigor of Fluther, but not all his philosophy. She has a son in France in the Dublin Fusiliers, and "never had no thruck with anything spotted by th' fingers o' th' Fenians," but yet it is she who goes for the doctor and who is shot dead while dragging the poor mad Nora from a position of danger. Miss Maureen Delany gave a very fine interpretation of the part and those of us who remember her chiefly as a comic actress must welcome her to tragedy. Bessie is the greatest heroine that Mr. O'Casey has yet created: she has even a greater personality than Juno. Miss Craig as the doleful Mrs. Gogan gave a fine performance and so did Miss Mooney as Rosie. Miss Shelah Richards as Nora Clitheroe gave the best performance we have ever seen her give: she was particularly convincing as the loving young wife in the first act. In the last, when she has lost her reason and forever imagines that she is in the country with Jack, Miss Richards showed that she has a great fund of tragic power. The play, in spite of its many men characters, centres chiefly in the women, and Mr. O'Casey shows us the woman's side of war. It is significant that he does not bring on to the stage the woman rebel fighter: he prefers to draw his lesson of humanity and charity from the great-hearted Bessie or the pitiful Nora.

There is no doubt that the audience of last Monday welcomed this new work of Mr. O'Casey: we have rarely seen an audience more moved than in the last act. And yet many were the peals of laughter in the earlier acts at Fluther's sallies.

W. S. [14]

The reviewer for the *Voice of Labour* was disturbed by the play. O'Casey had indicted war in a manner never before seen on an Abbey stage and this had appealed to labor's age-old hatred of death and destruction. Yet the 1916 Rising was impeached by a group of characters who were unmistakably of the working class—whom the *Voice of Labour* claimed to represent—and the martyrdom of Pearse and James Connolly all of a sudden didn't seem as clear as the trade union movement had made it.

> ... Trade languishes and our economic experts fill the columns of our morning papers with their forebodings. But the Abbey Theatre thrives upon the dramatic fare of Mr. Sean O'Casey after so many years of financial penury. Rumours of a new play by him formed part of the intimate gossip of Dublin for several weeks past; and, as a result, the early booking at the theatre became remarkable.
>
> On Monday night last, before a packed and enthusiastic house, *The Plough and the Stars*, a tragedy in four acts, was produced. Dealing with the Easter rebellion and the year preceding it, Mr. O'Casey brings to his theme the same dramatic strength and treatment which characterises all his work. *The Plough and the Stars* is in some ways a better play than *Juno*. It is a vital piece of drama, though its tragedy is less intense and its humorous spells more frequent than those of the earlier play. Mr. O'Casey has blunted the edge of that strange cynicism which hurts the mind in his other plays. He has shed a little of his love of theatricality. But his new play is as loosely woven as *Juno*. The humour is better; the dramatic cohesion is stronger. The interplay of tragedy and humour is not so pronounced—

that terrible ebb and flow which made *Juno* too vital a play for me. In *Juno,* strangest of all dramatic textures, the mind is given little peace, so intense is the pace of the action. But in *The Plough and the Stars* the action is more natural and less clamorous. The tragedy is held in check until the last act, when we receive it all. Nevertheless, the intention of the dramatist appears to have been otherwise. The consumptive child, Mollser, was evidently put into the play to re-act against the humour, but in that Mr. O'Casey failed. Mollser remains somewhat artificial and fails to haunt the acts of the play, a purpose for which I think she was intended.

MALEDICTION AND PRAYER

There is a restless spirit in this tragedy, one that is not too sure of what it believes or disbelieves; and this uncertainty takes away from the strength of the play, though one is apt to lose thought of it, so often and so frequently comes those moments that drench the dialogue with golden humour. In the last act the dying woman, Bessie Burgess, after giving of herself unsparingly to her women folk, mingles malediction and prayer in her last moments. She typifies the mood of the dramatist in this play and in *Juno.* Many of his characters betray this strange contrariness and temperament. His loafers become heroic, his heroes turn out cowards. In the third act of *The Plough and the Stars* Captain Brennan will not desert a wounded comrade. In the next act he discards his uniform, deserts his comrades, and becomes a fugitive flying from fear. Mr. O'Casey tries hard to explain this uncertainty, especially through the lips of Nora Clitheroe. But though he convinces us of her tragedy and the tragedy of her kind, he fails to explain away the actions or beliefs of his men characters.

THE SECOND ACT

There is much that is unforgettable in *The Plough and the Stars*; there is much that is unforgivable. The second act comes near spoiling the play, and could be dispensed with. The scene is a publichouse; the time, 1915. Here Irish nationalism adds to its fervour by drink, and those outside the movement satirise it—prostitute, communist, loafer, and others. Between the cross-talk and loose satire, a voice, speaking off the stage, using the well-beloved nationalism of Pearse, anticipates the rebellion of 1916. The dramatic effect is a terrible one; more terrible when one remembers that one is Irish. I waited till the close of the act for some justification of the use of sentences that were and are still part of our spiritual and national life. I did not find it. Mr. O'Casey's purpose I can understand, but cannot accept the consequences. To place in antagonism a nobility and a degeneracy is a theme for a genius, and none but a genius could bridge the gulf, killing viciousness and incongruity. The dramatist failed to do that.

Rosie Redmond, a woman of the streets, is used to intensify that antagonism, as is also the quarrel between the tenement women. She comes into the play at the second act, and with the close of the act she passes out of the play. She hardly justifies her introduction. She is, at best, a theatricality. The nationalism of Pearse may have fallen amongst strange companions in the days that witnessed its first manifestations, but it never lost its nobility. Mr. O'Casey, whatever his purpose may be, takes away that, an unforgivable thing. An Irish audience may one day turn away from this play because of that. Our cynicism will not always last.

POVERTY AND WAR

The dramatic greatness of Mr. O'Casey lies more in ability to create a community than in the making of one or more dominant characters. Within the narrow confines of narrow street and shabby tenement his people re-act against each other; but their hate, like their love, is instinctive rather than deep-rooted. Poverty and ill-health alone make them bitter of soul and tongue. But the evil they do to each other in everyday life is momentary, and ends with the day, quickly forgotten. Moments of common danger dissolve their prejudices and their dislikes. It is left to influences outside their lives to create the final and terrible disintegration. Caught in the vortex of a national anger, the men become heroes because they fear to be called cowards, and their women struggle against that untruth, fighting for their love and their homes. "I have sacrificed more for my love than they for their hate," Nora Clitheroe cries out when her husband leaves her to take his place among the insurgents.

Mr. O'Casey indicts war because it is only the poor who give all and receive nothing. Death, insanity, child-murder, are the inevitable consequences. Who gains by it all we do not know, nor do we want to. We only know that poverty pays the full price. In *The Plough and the Stars* humanity's cry against that price is a lyrical one. . . .[15]

Saturday's performances ended the play's one-week run, and its closing reception was reminiscent of opening night:

NO OPPOSITION
MR. O'CASEY GETS OVATION AT ABBEY

The matinee and night performances of Mr. Sean O'Casey's new play at the Abbey Theatre on Saturday were very well received by large audiences. At the conclusion of each performance the artists were loudly applauded, and were twice recalled. After the night performance Mr. O'Casey, in response to insistent demands from the audience, appeared on the stage and received an ovation. No opposition of any kind was manifested.[16]

Lady Gregory attended the Friday and Saturday night performances. On Sunday she recorded her reactions to the protests and to the play:

Feb. 14, Sunday. On Friday I left for Dublin to see *The Plough and the Stars*. I got the post and papers in Gort and when the train had started opened the *Independent* and saw a heading right across the page, "Riotous Scenes at the Abbey, Attempt to stop O'Casey's play," and an account of wild women, especially, having raised a disturbance, blown whistles, etc., prevented the second act from being heard and had then clambered on to the stage—a young man had struck Miss Delany on the face, etc, etc. Then the police had been sent for, and quiet apparently restored for the rest of the play to be given. It is so lucky I had set out and not seen this, at Coole, when too late to take the train.

At Athenry I got the *Irish Times*, which gave a fuller account. Yeats had spoken from the stage but the clamour had drowned his speech, but the reporters had got some of it. The train was very crowded, groups of men getting in at each station. I thought at first there must be a fair going on, but they were going up for the football, England v. Ireland, next day.

Yeats met me at the station and gave his account of the row; thought of inviting the disturbers to a debate as we had done in the *Playboy* riots, but I was against that. In *Playboy* time our opponents were men. They had a definite objective, they thought the countrypeople were being injured by Synge's representation of them. These disturbers were almost all women who have made demonstrations on Poppy Day and at elections and meetings; have made a habit of it, of the excitement.

We found the Abbey crowded, many being turned away. Yeats said that last night he had been there by accident, for he does not often go to more than one performance. Robinson had not come that evening and when the disturbance began and he wanted to call for police he found it was Perrin's night off and the telephone had been closed up. But at last the Civic Guards came and carried the women off the stage and the play went on without interruption to the end. At the end of the second act, a good many people had thought it was not to be resumed and had gone, and the disturbers had seized their places and kept up the noise from there, while some climbed on to the stage breaking two lamps and tearing a piece out of the curtain and attacked the actresses.

The papers said Miss Delany had been struck on the face by a young man. But the actors said he came next morning, very indignant at the accusation, said he had thrown something at Seaghan [Sean] Barlow* and it had accidentally hit Miss Craig. Miss Richards says she herself threw a shoe at one of the intruders and it missed its aim and one of them took it up and threw it at Yeats, but it then also missed its aim. I went round to see them in the Green-room and they were very cheerful. There was no attempt at disturbance, though one man said from the gallery, in the public-house scene, "This is an insult to the memory of Pearse," and walked out. Someone else cried out when two men of the Citizen Army came into the pub, one holding the flag of the Republic, the other of the Citizen Army—the Plough and Stars flag—it was designed by "A.E."—"Those flags were never in a public-house!" And it is natural they might object to that, though they don't know that scenes can't be re-arranged for every episode—the flags had to be shown and that scene was the most convenient.

And their bearers did but take a modest glass at the bar, and carried the flags out again with decency and order.

I thought the play very fine indeed. And the next day at the matinee, when, though the house was full and overflowing, there was no danger of riot and I could listen without distraction, it seemed to me a very wonderful play—"the forgiveness of sins," as real literature is supposed to be. These quarrelling, drinking women have tenderness and courage, showing all through, as have the men. At intervals in the public-house scene one hears from the meeting being held outside fragments of a speech of Pearse (spoken in Stephenson's fine voice with extraordinary effect). One feels those who heard it were forced to obey its call, not to be afraid to fight even in the face of defeat. One honours and understands their emotions. Lionel Johnson's lines to Ireland came into my mind:

> "For thy dead is grief on thee?
> Can it be thou dost repent
> That they went, thy chivalry
> Those sad ways magnificent?"

And then comes what all nations have seen, the suffering that falls through war, and especially civil war, on the women, the poor, the wretched homes and families of the slums. An overpowering play. I felt at the end of it as if I should never care to look at another; all others would seem so shadowy to the mind after this.

I saw it again in the evening, but too tired then to feel much emotion. The immense audience all applauding, and Casey was called at the end with the players and cheered.

The morning's excitement had been an attempt to kidnap Fitzgerald, "Fluther," the chief actor in the play. A motor with armed men had come to his house and demanded to see him. But he was not there; someone had said he now lived elsewhere, but when I spoke of it he told me he had not gone home that night, had some little suspicion in his mind. I said, if taken, he would now be wandering in the Wicklow mountains like some man who has lately been carried off.

It was thought safer for the players to stay in the Theatre between matinée and evening performance. So there was a meal made ready for them. And G. Yeats [Yeats's wife] brought Rummel, who had been giving a concert, and he played for the actors in the auditorium Chopin and Beethoven's Moonlight Sonata. Yeats fell asleep and awaking said he had dreamed there was a storm going on, and when he saw Rummel playing his last chords he thought "they can't have noticed it." The players were delighted. Rummel had arrived on Saturday morning for his concert. There was a great crush in the boat and he could not get a cabin until he happened to say he was coming over to play, and then he was given a cabin at once, he thought from respect for music, but found they thought he was one of the English football team![17]

3
Vox Litteratoris

> 2000 doctors are looking for work in the Irish Free State. And yet the Abbey Directors decided not to put on the "Plough and the Stars" for that second week.
> —*Dublin Opinion*

There is little doubt that *The Plough and the Stars* would have continued to fill the Abbey Theatre to capacity had the production continued. However, the drama now shifted from the theatre to the newspapers. "Letters to the Editor" appeared in Monday editions of nearly all the Dublin papers. The most prominent letter was from Mrs. Hannah Sheehy-Skeffington, leader of the protesters, to the *Irish Independent*.

> Your editorial misses what was apparent in your report regarding the Abbey Theatre protest. The demonstration was not directed against the individual actor, nor was it directed to the moral aspect of the play. It was on national grounds solely, voicing a passionate indignation against the outrage of a drama staged in a supposedly national theatre, which held up to derision and obloquy the men and women of Easter Week.
> The protest was made, not by Republicans alone, and had the sympathy of large numbers in the house. There is a point beyond which toleration becomes mere servility, and realism

not art, but morbid perversity. The play, as a play, may be left to the judgement of posterity, which will rank it as artistically far below some of Mr. O'Casey's work. It is the realism that would paint not only the wart on Cromwell's nose, but that would add carbuncles and running sores in a reaction against idealisation. In no country save in Ireland could a State-subsidised theatre presume on popular patience to the extent of making a mockery and a byword of a revolutionary movement on which the present structure claims to stand.

I am one of those who have gone for over twenty years to performances at the Abbey, and I admire the earlier ideals of the place that produced *Cathleen ni Houlihan*; that sent Sean Connolly out on Easter Week; that was later the subject of a British "Royal" Commission; the Abbey, in short, that helped to make Easter Week, and that now in its subsidised, sleek old age jeers at its former enthusiasms.

The incident, will, no doubt, help to fill houses in London with audiences that come to mock at those "foolish dead," whose names will be remembered forever.

The only censorship that is justified is the free censorship of public opinion. The Ireland that remembers with tear-dimmed eyes all that Easter Week stands for, will not, and cannot be silent in face of such a challenge.[1]

O'Casey's answer was not long coming.

A space please, to breathe a few remarks opposing the screams and the patter antagonistic to the performance of *The Plough and the Stars* in the Abbey Theatre. In her letter to the *Independent* Mrs. Sheehy-Skeffington does not drag before us the parts of the play that spread irritating thoughts over the minds of herself and her allies, but a talk with some of the young Republican women, which I had after the disturbance, enabled me to discover that the National tocsin of alarm was sounded because some of the tinsel of sham was shaken from the body of truth.

They objected to Volunteers and men of the I.C.A. visiting a public-house. Do they want us to believe that all these men were sworn teetotalers? Are we to know the fighters of Easter Week as "The Army of the Unco Guid"? Were all Ireland's battles fought by Confraternity men? The Staff of Stonewall Jackson complained bitterly to him of the impiety of one of their number. "A blasphemous scoundrel," said the General, "but a damned fine Artillery officer." Some of the men of Easter Week liked a bottle of stout, and I can see nothing derogatory in that.

They objected to the display of the tricolour, saying that that flag was never in a public-house. I myself have seen it there. I have seen it painted on a lavatory in "The Gloucester Diamond"; it has been flown from some of the worst slums in Dublin; I have seen it thrust itself from the window of a shebeen [an illegal pub] in "The Digs," but, perhaps the funniest use it was put to was when it was made to function as a State robe for the Mayor of Waterford.

They murmured against the viewpoint of "Nora Clitheroe," saying it did not represent the feeling of Ireland's womanhood. Nora voices not only the feeling of Ireland's women, but the women of the human race. The safety of her brood is the true morality of every woman. A mother does not like her son to be killed—she does not even like him to get married.

The Republican women shouted with a loud voice against the representation of fear in the eyes of the fighters. If this be so, what is the use of sounding forth their praises? If they knew no fear, then the fight of Easter Week was an easy thing, and those who participated deserve to be forgotten in a day, rather than to be remembered forever. And why is the sentiment expressed in *The Plough and the Stars* condemned, while it goes unnoticed (apparently) in other plays? In *The Old Man* (written by a Republican) during a crisis, the many fall back; only the few press forward. In *Sable and Gold* (played by the Republican Players) a Volunteer, who is a definite coward, is one of the principal characters, and yet no howl has proclaimed the representation to be false or defaming. And are the men of Easter Week greater than those whose example they are said to have followed? Were they all unhuman in that they were destitute of the first element in the nature of man? "Upon the earth there is not his like," says Job, "who is made without fear." Even the valiant Hector, mad with fear, was chased around the walls of Troy. And do the Republicans forget the whisper of [Robert] Emmet to the question of the executioner, "Are you ready, sir?"—"Not yet, not yet." I wonder do the Republicans remember how Laoghaire and Conall, two of the champions of the Red Branch, ran, as rabbits would run, from what they believed to be the certainty of death; and how Cuchulain alone remained to face death, with "pale countenance, drooping head, in the heaviness of dark sorrow"?

One of the young Republicans whispered to me in admiration the name of Shaw, inferentially to my own shame and confusion. Curious champion to choose, and I can only attribute their choice to ignorance; for if ever a man hated sham, it is Shaw. Let me give one example that concerns the subject I am writing about. Describing in *Arms and the Man*, a charge of cavalry, Bluntschli says: "It's like slinging a handful of peas against a windowpane; first one comes; then two or three close behind him; then all the rest in a lump." Then Raina answers, with dilating eyes (how like a young Republican woman!) "Yes, first one! the bravest of the brave!" followed by the terrible reply: "H'm; you should see the poor devil pulling at his horse!"

As for vanity, I think I remember a long discussion in *The Volunteer* over the adoption of the green and gold, scarlet and blue, black, white, and crimson-plumed costumes of the Volunteers of '82 for the Volunteers of '13; and though these were rejected—they had to be—there was still left a good deal of boyish vanity in the distribution of braids, tabs, slung swords, and Sam Browne belts. And how rich (to me) was the parade of the stiff and stately uniformed men, "the solemn-looking dials of them," as Rosie Redmond says in the play—and they marching to the meeting were, very human, but damnably funny.

I am glad that Mrs. Sheehy-Skeffington says that the demonstration was not directed against any individual actor. As Mr. F. J. McCormick told the audience, the author alone is responsible for the play, and he is willing to take it all. The politicians—Free State and Republican—have the platform to express themselves, and Heaven knows they seem to take full advantage of it. The drama is my place for self-expression, and I claim the liberty in drama that they enjoy on the platform (and how they enjoy it!), and am prepared to fight for it.

The heavy-hearted expression by Mrs. Sheehy-Skeffington about "the Ireland that remembers with tear-dimmed eyes all that Easter Week stands for, " makes me sick. Some of the men cannot get even a job. Mrs. Skeffington is certainly not dumb, but she appears to be both blind and deaf to all the things that are happening around her. Is the Ireland that is pouring to the picture-houses, to the dance halls, to the football matches, remembering with tear-dimmed eyes all that Easter Week stands for. Tears may be in the eyes of the navvies working on the Shannon scheme [an electrification project on the River Shannon], but they are not for Ireland. When Mrs. Skeffington roars herself into the position of a dramatic critic, we cannot take her seriously: she is singing here on a high note wildly beyond the range of her political voice, and can be given only the charity of our silence.

In refutation of a story going around, let me say that there never was a question of a refusal to play the part of "Rosie Redmond" (splendidly acted by Miss Mooney). The part declined by one of the players was the character of "Mrs. Gogan."

I have no intention of noticing the poor stupid things written by the Kellys, Burkes, Sheas, and the Finigans.

Sean O'Casey[2]

Other letters appeared, including a few from O'Casey's "Kellys, Burkes, [and] Sheas."

I do not profess to be a dramatic critic and I endeavour to be strictly non-political. On Wednesday night last I visited the Abbey Theatre, and I came away, like Mr. Collins, very disappointed indeed. The play was very mediocre, richly flavoured with vulgarity and profanity, much of which could be dispensed with without detracting from its merits.

For instance, why introduce a prostitute in the second act? I venture to suggest she was thrown in to make good weight; certainly she did not form a connecting link in the "plot," as we saw no more of her in the succeeding acts.

Still, I see no good reasons why objection should be taken on political grounds. Offence was not given to any party whatever; in fact, the whole piece could be construed to laud the actions of the brave men of the Citizen Army.

I certainly cannot agree that the play is "the work of a genius," as Senator Yeats has described it, for in the hands of other than the very capable Abbey Players I believe the whole thing would be an absolute failure.

John McQueen
37 Blessington Street

In the name of those who gave their lives for Ireland in Easter Week, 1916, I protest against the scurrilous insinuation in "The Plough and the Stars".

Senator W. B. Yeats has, indeed, taken an important role on himself when he dictates Mussolini-like, to a Dublin audience. Because a "shoneen" clique in the Abbey following boost Sean O'Casey, we are all to give him and his works a triumphant reception.

As one who was fortunate enough to take part in that most glorious episode of Irish history which laid the foundations of the present State, I give the lie to the suggestions of O'Casey that those who fought had no ideals, were cowards and buffoons. Lastly, our women—wives, sisters, and mothers—were a source of inspiration to our men during the revolt and urged them on—not hindering them.

Sean O'Shea
Trafalgar Terrace
Monkstown[3]

On the day the letters appeared, O'Casey and John Lyle Donaghy,* a young poet and supporter of O'Casey, visited Lady Gregory. Her account of the visit gives us another picture of Holloway and of the trouble O'Casey was having with his eyes.

Feb. 15. Donaghy came in as I was writing and we had a long talk. He is full of ideas and plans, hopes to have some of his poems published soon, to take his degree in June, and then to go to London, try his hand at literature, perhaps acting. He is working at the translation of Prometheus. He was wearing a heavy ulster and I asked if he would not take it off, but he said, No, there was a large rent in his coat, gained in "the celebrations" last night of the football victory.

He had been at the Abbey the night of the riot, had seen the first attack on the stage, a woman climbing up on it, and then the ferocious face of Seaghan Barlow, almost petrified with astonishment at *his* stage being invaded, and who had then stepped forward and flung the invader off it. Donaghy had met Holloway in the hall, in a state of fury—"An abominable play."

D.: "I see nothing abominable in it."
H.: "Then you have a dirty mind."
D.: "No. I haven't."
H.: "Well, you have a filthy mind. There are no street-walkers in Dublin."
D.: "I was accosted by one only last night."
H.: "There were none in Dublin till the Tommies brought them over."

Then H. said to a man coming down from the gallery, "That play should be put off the stage."

But he answered, "No. It should not."

I ran round to see the Yeats children and W. [illie?] showed me *The Observer* account of the riot. Then to the cafe where I had O'Casey and Donaghy to tea, Casey in good spirits after his reception last night. One of the objections made was the rebel flag having been carried into a public-house, but two old I.R.A. men have since told him that they themselves had brought the flag into pubs. He reminded some of the men who objected to a street-walker having been put on, how often they had received food and shelter from these women when being hunted by the Black-and-Tans.

He stayed talking till near 8 o'clock, has his mind full of plays, too full perhaps, but his eyes have been very troublesome again. He has a difficulty in typing what he has written. His doctor says he must get a better lodging where he can have his food cooked for him, for he is indolent about doing it himself and is letting down his strength. One of the accusations of the interrupters had been that he did not make the Tommies offensive enough. But he says they were usually quite civil until they were frightened and turned cruel. They would come into the house and say "Mother, give us some tea," or whatever they wanted.[4]

The *Irish Statesman* continued its coverage of the controversy, publishing a reassessed review of the play and letters from Liam O'Flaherty and Austin Clarke,* two of Ireland's noted authors. The review, by "Spectator," found mixed blessings from the disturbances and made a feeble attempt to gauge the literary merits of the play.

POLITICS AND PEOPLE

It was my luck to see *The Plough and the Stars* the day after the fair, or, should it be, the fun? Anyway, the only echo at the Friday performance of all the tumult that had been was a mild and rather deprecating voice protesting that "the tricolour was never seen in a publichouse." I was amused to discover that the offending standard-bearer was Mr. Arthur Shields, who was in the G.P.O. in Easter Week, and I am prepared to bet he recognised a few old comrades amongst the mob who attempted to storm the stage. Mr. O'Casey, I suspect, was too subtle for his interrupters, who apparently were blind to the significance of the fact that whereas hangers-on like the Fluther and his friends ran lavishly to "balls of malt," each of the three Volunteers limited himself to one harmless "small port." Dramatically I don't see much is gained by bringing in the flags, though it is fantastically absurd to suggest it was intended as an insult. The incident is obviously a rather crude device to let Clitheroe make an appearance in this scene, and also to indicate, as Mr. O'Casey might easily have done in the opening act, the alliance between the National Volunteers and the Citizen Army.

Personally I cannot help feeling grateful as a playgoer to Mrs. Sheehy-Skeffington and her friends. In the Friday calm that followed Thursday's brief typhoon, I heard for the first time an O'Casey play without losing half the good things of the dialogue through the senseless guffaws of a section of the audience. If his opponents did their best to spoil one night for Mr. O'Casey, his admirers have marred a hundred. I appreciated the strained attention of the audience all the more because in *The Plough and the Stars* Mr. O'Casey is attempting a new experiment in dialogue. His prose has never lacked energy and vividness, but in the other plays the speech of his characters kept close to the note of actual conversation. In this tragedy, without losing touch with life, he aims at subtler rhythms and more elaborate harmonies, and makes a good bid to show that the talk of the Dublin tenements can yield as rich possibilities as the speech of Aran fishers or Wicklow tramps. Mr. O'Casey does not seem to me to have quite pulled it off, largely, I think, because, unlike Synge, he has not yet succeeded in fusing words and action into unity. *The Plough and the Stars* develops at a speed with which the dialogue does not always keep pace, and it was not the fault of the players if the best of them gave the impression at times of being engaged in a verbal obstacle race.

Spectator[5]

Liam O'Flaherty's letter was a slashing attack on the play and revealed some surprising Social-Darwinist opinions from a writer whose brilliance was unquestioned. Only the year before, his masterful novel *The Informer* had been published.

To the Editor of the *Irish Statesman*

Dear Sir,—Permit me to protest in your columns against Mr. Yeats' demonstration in the Abbey Theatre on Thursday last. The protest by those who objected to the play (*The Plough and the Stars*) was undoubtedly in bad taste, but nobody loses anything by it, least of all the author, who gained a good advertisement. But the protest by Mr. Yeats, against the protest of the audience, was an insult to the people of this country. I feel that I am personally justified in protesting against his protest because the manner in which they have received my own work (and in all probability the manner in which they WILL receive my work) defends me from the accusation of appealing to the gallery. Allow me to review the position.

In my opinion, *The Plough and the Stars* is a bad play. It would be quite in order for an audience to hiss it as a bad play. It was, however, a boorish thing to hiss it because the opinions expressed by the author injured the feelings of the audience. Every man has a right to his opinions. Mr. O'Casey has a right to his opinions. He has a perfect right to protest himself against this treatment of his work by the audience. But Mr. Yeats had positively no right to strut forward and cry with joy that the people of this country had "been cut to the bone." Our people have their faults. It is a good thing that artists should point out these faults. But it is not a good thing that pompous fools should boast that we have been "cut to the bone."

I say WE, because I too was cut to the bone. I am not a Nationalist in the political sense. But I am an admirer of any man who has the courage to die for an ideal. And I think the most glorious gesture in the history of our country was the gesture of those who died in 1916. No great artist in any country in the world refused to give credit, to glorify men who died likewise. Even Tolstoy, the great pacifist, bowed down before the courage of the Cossacks and of their brigand enemies (even brigands) who died with their death-song on their lips. I bow down before the courage of Pearse and Connolly and their comrades. I did not have the honour to fight with them. But I "am cut to the bone" because an Irish writer did not, unfortunately, do them justice. I do not blame O'Casey. I believe him to be a sincere man. But I am sorry to see him defended by a man who rose to fame on the shoulders of those men who stirred this country to fervent enthusiasm for ideals in the last generation. What does it matter to us whether these ideals were practical? No ideal is practical, but all ideals are the mothers of great poetry, and it is only from the womb of an ideal that a great race, or a great literature, or a great art can spring.

I am not "cut to the bone" because the play was not anti-English. I fervently admire the English race. I envy the English race for their greatness, for their bravery, for the great men they have produced. I envy their Cromwells, their Shakespeares, their Shelleys, their Darwins, their countless heroes who have struggled for the English ideal, whether it be a Wat Tyler or a Frobisher, a Clive or a William Morris. The great poetry of life is the struggle of brave men. And the contemptible thing in life is the strutting of pompous people who spit at the justified anger of enthusiasts. "Let him who is without sin cast the first stone."

Sir, I am of Gaelic stock. My ancestors came into this country sword in hand, as conquerors, as the Danes came and the Normans and the English. To conquer is the right of the strong. We who conquered once have been in turn conquered. I acclaim our conquerors. But now the conquered and the conquerors are one. And out of their seed another race has sprung. We are all brothers. All but those who turn their backs on their people and cry, spitting, that they "have been cut to the bone." It was not so that [Henry Joy] McCracken cried, or [Theobald Wolfe] Tone,* or [Robert] Emmet,* or even the great Parnell.

Finally, I do not believe in political nationalism. I do not believe in Empires. The human race has advanced considerably since the time of Daithí and even since the time of Napoleon. I believe in the political union of the human race, in the ideal of human brotherhood. But there always will be strife and struggle. Soon perhaps that strife will be intellectual competition. But it is certain that always people born in one place will love that place and try to make it preeminent by the achievements of its people. And always brave men will love the weak and struggle with them. And always poets will side with the weak against the strong, and not with the strong against the weak and ignorant. And always great men will not become embittered, even as Synge did not become embittered, but smiled gently like a Christ at those who reviled him.—Yours faithfully,

Liam O'Flaherty
15 February 1926[6]

O'Casey was not without his supporters. Lyle Donaghy lashed out against O'Flaherty's hypocrisy.

To the Editor of the *Irish Statesman*

. . . There is a ripeness of time which the reformer must await, but that moment is not always the moment of popular sympathy and acclaim, which at least neither artist nor reformer need attend; and now, it seems to me that the time is ripe for a greater effort that the dream of all the poets may come into its own, when humanity shall not be divided against itself. The glory of the spirit in man may find expression in many ways. What poet ever scorned that glory, even when it expressed itself through the horrors of a bloody war? Of course Tolstoi did not; nor does Sean O'Casey; but must we, because men err bravely, put aside the truth which has forced itself upon us? The men of 1916 fought for an ideal. Is it to be said that when the streams flowed and horror stalked abroad, when they found themselves men capable of love and hate and fear, they sought to hide the truth from themselves, and that there were none among them like Captain Brennan? Had they lived to pass from ideal to deeper ideal, had they survived to survey the smoking ruins and assess the gains, I do not think that they would have been afraid to face the facts; neither was Sean O'Casey; neither is any artist.

It seems to me that Mr. O'Flaherty is false to the poet in himself; for I do not think that a true artist (such as I believe Mr. O'Flaherty to be) admits the impracticability of ideals. He is constituted to believe in them. Myself, I have worshipped ideals in the past, though rejecting the name, for that I believe true idealism to be in essence a far-sighted realism, and all true ideals practical. I feel that this unbelief in Mr. O'Flaherty has tainted his letter, which appears to hold up great lives as good because they produce great poetry, rather than poetry because it serves life. In fact, I shudder when I hear him speak of the 1916 battle as a gesture, for I feel that he is sinking to the posture more usually, though I think unfairly, attributed to Mr. Yeats, that attitude, adopting which one might wave a thousand to the scaffold for a symbol's sake, when the end of existence, no longer an unknown good, is content to be a temporary pose.

Alas, it is only such a posture that could give way to the tenet that the most exalted strife of the future will be an intellectual competition. Yet such I deduce is Mr. O'Flaherty's belief. Had he used the word "competition," meaning thereby "to seek in company with" or "to contend together for an ultimate good in which all may share," then, though it is a postclassic word, I would have taken my hat off to him that used it; but I fear it is not so, and that I must wait until my mind has further developed or my youth has departed, or Mr. O'Flaherty has advanced his standard, whether in public house or palace, before I can shake hands with him on the subject.—Yours faithfully,

Lyle Donaghy[7]

Gabriel Fallon, one of the actors in the play, and Herbert Palmer, describing himself as a "nondescript outsider," also answered O'Flaherty.

To the Editor of the *Irish Statesman*

Dear Sir,—Under *The Plough and the Stars* Mr. O'Flaherty talks of many things, and talks of them so breathlessly as to make one believe that it must have been impossible for him, his indignation spent, to know exactly what he, Mr. O'Flaherty, was talking about.

Mr. Yeats' remark that "it appeared that O'Casey had cut to the bone" was made to the players in the Green Room of the Abbey Theatre and was not made in the manner suggested by Mr. O'Flaherty.

It is Mr. O'Flaherty's opinion that *The Plough and the Stars* is a bad play and that O'Casey did not do justice to the men who died in 1916.

This is all that matters in Mr. O'Flaherty's letter.

As for the rest, neither Mr. O'Flaherty's fighting ancestry nor his far-flung beliefs can have any interest for those interested in *The Plough and the Stars.*—Yours faithfully,

Gabriel J. Fallon

To the Editor of the *Irish Statesman*

Dear Sir.—Would you allow a nondescript outsider to say a little thing. I like Liam O'Flaherty's letter on The Plough and the Stars. . . . I thought parts of it very gallant, in spite of its swagger. Unfortunately I have not seen O'Casey's play, which I imagine (from what I have read about it) I should have liked even better than the letter, and entirely agreed with Mr. Yeats. But one passage in the letter rather startled me; it was this: "But Mr. Yeats had positively no right to strut forward and cry with joy that the people of this country had been 'cut to the bone.' Our people have their faults. It is a good thing that artists should point out their faults. But it is not a good thing that pompous fools should boast that we have been 'cut to the bone.' "

What I chiefly want to say is this: Liam O'Flaherty in that passage is imposing upon the generosity of his own people. I think, in spite of his fighting ancestry, he dare not write such a passage in an English journal about any powerful English literary celebrity. No English artist, although it avoids the libellous, could write such a passage in an English journal about a powerful literary celebrity (especially if the latter were in touch with coteries and cliques) without paying heavily for it. This may be a burning shame; but during the last years it has been true. I speak from personal experience.—Yours faithfully,

Herbert E. Palmer
22 Batchwood View,
St. Albans[8]

In the same issue as the O'Flaherty letter was a message from Austin Clarke, one of Ireland's better poets. Clarke found O'Casey's technique "moribund" and exploitive of "our" poorer people. Clarke was living in London at the time.

To the Editor of the *Irish Statesman*

Dear sir,—May I suggest that in the interests of Irish art the Abbey Theatre be regarded as merely another "lovers' quarrel"? Many of the old Anglo-Irish school have been inclined to think that only a work of genius can cause disturbance. "The Playboy" was mistaken for a picture of our western people, but, moving in its own rich world of poetry and realistic phantasy, it endures. A bad topical play, run flagrantly in the interests of the party politics of the moment, might give offence, yet remain a bad play. Owing to the strong anti-Irish prejudice in this country, any play that merely belittled our people would be popular, and it is therefore imperative that the question of art should come first. Several writers of the new Irish school believe that Mr. O'Casey's work is a crude exploitation of our poorer people in an Anglo-Irish tradition that is now moribund. Frank discussion can alone bring us the truth. May one hope that your paper, ignoring the recent revival of Anglo-Irish coterie criticism, which is doing so much harm to our art, will open its columns to the discussion of the artistic values in dispute?—Yours faithfully,

Austin Clarke
London[9]

Clarke found support from F. R. Higgins, the poet, who had little use for the play and offered his own analysis of the controversy.

To the Editor of the *Irish Statesman*

Dear Sir,—From the controversy appearing in your columns regarding an interpretation of Mr. Sean O'Casey's recent tragedy, it is quite evident that the main questions at issue are merely based upon a revival of that arrogance of the

Gall [Irish for "foreigner"], recently dormant, towards the Gael. Personally, I consider that arrogance beside the point. Now that some have forgotten the cold logic of *Sixteen Dead Men* and their influence on those

"That converse bone to bone"

and of a time when

"A terrible beauty is born,"

let the bone be left to those who first snarled over it.

It is rather interesting to note that none of Mr. O'Casey's defenders have taken up the suggestion made by Mr. Austin Clarke that *The Plough and the Stars* should be considered primarily from an art standard. Mr. Yeats and AE saved poetry and the drama from political rhetoric and it is strange that, notwithstanding the "dedavisiation" [probably a reference to Thomas Davis, nineteenth-century Irish poet] of the stage, a new political creed is the only quality for which Mr. O'Casey is offered applause.

One is eager to have the opinions of our dramatic critics on a technique largely based upon the revue structure, in the quintessence of an all-Abbey burlesque, intensified by "divarsions" and Handy Andy incidents, with the original settings offered by Sean O'Casey. That aspect of comedy so gushly over-portrayed from Dublin artisan life, as seen only by this playwright, merely affords laborious bowing on a one-string fiddle—and "Fluther" Good's is just the successor of Captain Boyle's more lively rag-time.

Mr. Sean O'Casey, in his new play, entirely lacks the sincerity of an artist. One, of course, is frankly suspicious of reputations largely advertised by such a slogan as "docker dramatist"—the artist can only be judged by his work and as an artist he is beside his class—this label is just the condescension of intellectual snobbery. If, as a sincere artist, Mr. O'Casey interpreted the raw life he is supposed to know, the sure strokes of a great dramatist would have painted such a picture of the Dublin underworld that instead of driving some to demolish the theatre, they would be driven out in horror to abolish the slum. Yours truly,

F. R. Higgins
Rathfarnham[10]

The *Voice of Labour* also reassessed its position in light of the protests. It did not matter whether or not O'Casey was a "docker-dramatist." What mattered was that he was identified with the early labor movement, a period associated with the greatness and power of James Larkin. Cathal Shannon, editor of the *Voice*, was a bitter opponent of Larkin; Larkin had returned from the United States in 1923, and his militancy was a threat to Shannon's bureaucratic unionism. It was well known that O'Casey was a friend and comrade of Larkin. An attack on O'Casey was, therefore, an attack on that earlier period. It was no accident, then, that the *Voice* resurrected O'Casey's past.

After a column and a half of suggestions that the Free State government employ Irish artists and writers "to publish our glories abroad to the world," the writer, Tommy Irwin, showed why the Irish labor movement was in such a morass.

... AT THE ABBEY

The passages we have quoted were recalled to our mind by some recent incidents in Dublin. We refer in particular to the violent protest which a section of the audience made last week at one of the performances of "The Plough and the Stars." Let us add at once that we do not agree with the method the protesters adopted nor with the attempt to keep Mr. Barry Fitzgerald away from the theatre on Saturday. Indeed, of all the people concerned the actors and actresses have most of our sympathy. Nor can we be accused of prejudice against the Abbey Theatre, for the friendly interest of this journal and the class it serves, in the work of the Abbey is one of the things of which the workers may, we humbly believe, be very proud. But there are certain circumstances in connection with "The Plough and the Stars" which should be understood and which should have been known to the directors of the theatre. The exercise of the faculties of observation and memory might have prevented some of the trouble.

OUT OF THE PAST

We can easily understand that many in Dublin should resent portions of the play. In a few weeks time they will be celebrating the tenth anniversary of one of the noblest as it was one of the most daring adventures in our history. In those ten years the people of Ireland have gone through wars and revolutions and sufferings unexperienced in the memory of the living generation in this country. While the people are now shedding—and rightly shedding—many of their illusions, it should not be forgotten that this is Ireland still and that memories of the dead persist and are dear to large numbers of us. To associate those dead with a scene and in circumstances that the critics agree add nothing to the action of the play may have been a clever and effective piece of juggling, but it is not going to be appreciated as good art by the ordinary, common folk of this island.

AN EVIL MEMORY

The dramatist's own connection with the period of his play was not likely to be forgotten either. That connection may not be within the memory or the observation of the Abbey directorate, but it assuredly was well known to many who either took part in the events of Easter Week or knew the chief actors therein or some of the dead caricatured in the play. We don't believe the objectors would say that Sean O'Casey should have fought in Easter Week or that he should have remained in the ranks of the Irish Citizen Army after the winter of 1914-1915. But his connection with internal events in the I.C.A. when the late James Connolly was preparing that body for armed revolution should have made him the last person to have the impudence to stage what he did stage, and as Dublin is a city of whispers it was too much to be expected that the whole body of Abbey patrons should not be aware that before the actual performance the city was full of the rumour that what has become known as "soldiers' language" was not conspicuous in the first draft of the play by its absence. All this may not accord with the tenets of the devotees of high art. But this is Ireland in 1926, not Utopia.

ANOTHER YEATS

While we are saying so much we may refer to a remark dropped by Senator W. B. Yeats in his speech in the Abbey when he lectured the protestors as if he were their schoolmaster. "The Plough and the Stars" had cut very close to the bone, he said. It wasn't the only thing that has cut close to the bone of late. A few hundred yards from the Abbey Theatre a score or so of young men and women have been picketing a picture theatre and restaurant in which there has been an industrial dispute for the past seven or eight months. Does Senator Yeats not think that it cut very close to the bone when patrons of the Abbey watched Senator Yeats himself and his fellow-director, Mr. Lennox Robinson, march boldly past these pickets and into a picture show in this theatre? Does he not think it cut close to the bone—ay, and burned into the heart—when the pickets saw some of Dublin's leading artists go in and decorate that blackleg establishment and others, musicians, artists, professional men, refuse to use their influence to have the Nine Arts' Ball held elsewhere than in the Metropole? Verily this separating of the artist from the rest of this little world of Dublin, this "attempt among the artists to keep themselves apart as a wonderful and mysterious race," is very bad for the great brotherhood of art, for art itself, and for Dublin. Surely it would have been as well worth the while of the Abbey to look at real, hard, bitter realities a few hundred yards away in O'Connell Street as a few hundred yards away in Marlborough Street or Corporation Street? And is it not rather the sleek, well-fed people who guffaw so loudly of late in the Abbey who ought to be cut close to the bone? When an artist like Toller dealt with them he cut right to the marrow.[11]

O'Casey's answer was immediate and was printed along with the *Voice of Labour's* answer to it.

> The Abbey Theatre
> Dublin
> 20 February 1926
>
> Sir,—Permit me to correct a statement appearing in your paper connecting me with "internal events in the I.C.A. when the late James Connolly was preparing that body for armed revolution."
>
> I had no connection whatever, direct or indirect, with the

I.C.A. at that time: I had left, abandoned, deserted, fled from (take your choice of terms) the I.C.A. long before James Connolly had begun to "prepare that body for armed revolution."

Tommy Irwin asks "the author to show us the tenements in Dublin with the three-room flats." He knows of none. The original script has: "The home of the Clitheroes. It consists of the front and back drawing-rooms of a fine old Georgian house." The alteration was made to suit the limitations of the Abbey stage.

May I beg of you for God's sake, and for the reputation of the Irish Labour movement (such as it is) to prevent poor Tommy Irwin from framing his stupidities by trying to write about the Drama?

Sincerely yours,
Sean O'Casey

Mr. O'Casey denies one of several statements made in last week's VOICE OF LABOUR. But he was not able to deny his connection with a discreditable cabal against a prominent member of the I.C.A. while he was still a member of that organisation. Really, the particular moment at which his connection with the I.C.A. was ignobly severed doesn't matter, but at the time the late James Connolly *was* preparing for revolution. We can no more accept the statement of Mr. Sean O'Casey now than we did when the widow of the late Thomas J. Clarke was constrained by decency to write to the "Evening Telegraph" in March, 1918: "Mr. Sean O Cathasaigh makes the statement that Mr. P. T. Daly was an intimate friend of my husband (the late Tom Clarke) and Sean MacDermott up to their end. In making that statement Mr. O Cathasaigh must know that he states what is not the truth. . . . As to Mr. O Cathasaigh's boasted friendship and intimacy, well, so far as I know, it came to an abrupt end long before Easter, 1916." There is no difference between the O Cathasaigh of 1914 or 1918 and the O'Casey of 1926.

That a Dublin man who works and is a son of the tenements should write what he feels about a performance at the Abbey seems to have cut pretty close to the bone of a

genius at his apotheosis. It's too bad. Playwrights ought to be protected from workingmen in the Press, as they are (sometimes) from hostile demonstrations in the theatre. At all events, Tom Irwin has compelled the admission that at least one "alteration was made to suit the limitations of the Abbey stage." That isn't a bad achievement for a working-class critic. How many other changes—to suit the spirit of the Abbey directorate—were made the Abbey deities alone know.
Ed., VOICE OF LABOUR[12]

In the midst of the controversy, O'Casey wrote to Sara Allgood. Though, as he says, he was under doctor's orders to "do as little as possible," he was not to get a respite. Mrs. Sheehy-Skeffington was back with a longer and more in-depth attack on the play.

Dublin
23 February 1926

Dear Sally,

Sorry the run of "Juno" is ending, but the play had a fairly gay time of it.

I am still negotiating with Mr. [J. B.] Fagan about "The Plough and the Stars."

The play has raised something of a whirlwind in Dublin.

Am unable to write more: both of my eyes are very bad & painful. Doctor's orders to do as little as possible.

Best wishes,
Sean[13]

Sir,—In his letter Mr. O'Casey sets himself the task of replying to certain criticisms of his play. Since receiving Mr. Yeats's police-protected "apotheosis" Mr. O'Casey appears to take himself over-seriously, not sparing those of us who decline to bow the knee before his godhead. His play becomes "the shaking of the tinsel of sham from the body of truth"; an over-statement surely, for of the body of truth as portrayed in *The Plough and the Stars* one may only discern a leprous corpse.

As Arthur Griffith wrote nearly twenty years ago, when last police assisted at an Abbey production: "If squalidness, coarseness, and crime are to be found in Ireland, so are cancer, smallpox and policemen." But because these are to be found it would not be true to claim that nothing but these are present in Ireland. Because Mr. O'Casey has seen the tricolour painted on a lavatory wall he claims the right to parade it in a public-house as typical of the custom of the Citizen Army and the Volunteers. Because indecent and obscene inscriptions are similarly so found one may not exalt them as great literature.

Mr. O'Casey's original version, as is now generally known, was pruned before production. One wonders on what basis certain parts were excluded and others retained. This may, indeed, be the reason for the lopsidedness of some scenes, suffering, as sometimes the picture plays do, from a drastic, ill-concealed cut. Will the original version now appear in London and elsewhere, benefiting by the reclame of a "succes de scandale," a reclame that is usually ephemeral?

As to Mr. O'Casey's ransacking of literature to find soldiers that show fear or vanity, all that is beside the point. Whether the sight of men parading before an action that will lead many of them to their death is "damnable funny," or whether it might be pitiful and heart-rendering, is also a matter of presentment and point of view. The Greeks, who knew not Mr. O'Casey, used to require of a tragedy that it evoke feelings in the spectator of "pity and terror," and Shakespeare speaks of holding the "mirror up to nature." Submitted to either criteria, *The Plough and the Stars* is assuredly defective. But no doubt Mr. O'Casey would regard such standards as sadly out of date.

A play that deals with Easter Week and what led up to it, that finds in Pearse's words (spoken in almost his very accents) a theme merely for the drunken jibe of "dope," in which every character connected with the Citizen Army is a coward, a slacker, or worse, that omits no detail of squalid slumdom, the looting, the squabbling, the disease and degeneracy, yet that omits any revelation of the glory and the inspiration of Easter Week, is a *Hamlet* shown without the Prince of Denmark.

Is it merely a coincidence that the only soldiers whose knees do not knock together with fear and who are indifferent to the glories of their uniform are the Wiltshires? Shakespeare pandered to the prejudices of his time and country by representing Joan of Arc as a ribald, degraded campfollower. Could one imagine his play being received with enthusiasm in the French theatre of the time, subsidised by the State?

I learn that Mr. O'Casey's personal knowledge of the Citizen Army does not extend beyond 1914-15. To those, however, who remember the men and women of 1916 such presentation in a professedly "National" theatre seems a gross libel.

Mourning for the men of Easter Week is not incompatible with sympathy for the suffering survivors. The Ireland that is "pouring to the picture houses, the dance halls and the football matches" is the Ireland that forgets—that never knew. It is the Ireland that sits comfortably in the Abbey stalls and applauds Mr. O'Casey's play. It is the Ireland of the garrison, which sung twenty years ago "God Save the King" (while Mr. Yeats then, too, enforced the performance of *The Playboy* with the aid of the police). These do not shed tears for the navvy on the Shannon nor for the men of Easter Week nor for the sores of the slums.

Mr. O'Casey accords me as a critic in a shrieking paragraph or two the "charity of his silence." Unfortunately for his play, the professional critics are for the most part on my side, justifying my opinion that his latest play is also his poorest. For (pace Mr. Yeats) the police do not necessarily confer immortality, nor is it invariably a sign of a work of genius to be hissed by an Irish audience.

Arthur Griffith wrote thus in *Sinn Fein* of a similar episode:—"Mr. Yeats has struck a blow" (by calling in police and arresting certain members of the audience who protested against *The Playboy)* "at the freedom of the theatre in Ireland. It was perhaps the last freedom left to us. Hitherto, as in Paris or in Berlin or in Athens 2000 years ago, the audience in Ireland was free to express its opposition to a play. Mr. Yeats has denied this right. He has wounded both art and his country."

May I suggest that when Mr. O'Casey proceeds to lecture

us on "the true morality of every woman" he is somewhat beyond his depth. Nora Clitheroe is no more "typical of Irish womanhood" than her futile, sniveling husband is of Irish manhood. The women of Easter Week, as we know them, are typified in the mother of Padraic Pearse, that valiant woman who gave both her sons for freedom. Such breathe the spirit of Volumnia, or the Mother of the Gracchi.
That Mr. O'Casey is blind to it does not necessarily prove that it is non-existent, but merely that his vision is defective. That the ideals for which these men died have not been achieved does not lessen their glory nor make their sacrifices vain. "For they shall be remembered for ever" by the people if not by the Abbey directorate.[14]

O'Casey replied immediately.

26 February 1926

Sir: In a letter on the 15th inst. Mrs. Sheehy-Skeffington said that "the demonstration was not directed to the moral aspect of the play. It was on National grounds solely." Yet in her letter of 23rd she viciously affirms what she had before denied, and prancing out, flings her gauntlet in the face of what she calls the "obscenities and indecencies" of the play. She does more: in the righteousness of her indignation, she condemns, by presumption, what she has neither seen nor heard.

This is her interpretation of the Rights of Man. Evidently the children of National Light in their generation are as cute as the children of National Darkness by placing a puritanical prop under the expression of National dissatisfaction, even though the cuteness requires an action that can be called neither fair nor just.

We know as well as Mrs. Sheehy-Skeffington that obscene and indecent expressions do not make great literature, but we know, too, that great literature may make use of obscene and indecent expressions without altogether destroying its beauty and richness. She would hardly question the greatness in literature of Shakespeare (somebody a year or so ago wrote asking if Shakespeare wrote thirty plays without a naughty word, why couldn't O'Casey write them), but in the condemnation of an O'Casey play, the green cloak is concealed by the puritanical mantle. Indeed, her little crow over the possible horror of the censored part of the play seems to whisper that the wish is father to the thought, and that, when the play is published, nothing less (or more) will satisfy her than that the united church bells of Dublin, of their own accord, in a piercing peal will clang together—"This is a bad, bad, bad, bad play!"

There is no use of talking now of what Mr. Arthur Griffith thought of or wrote about *The Playboy*. Now the world thinks, and I think so, too, that *The Playboy* is a masterpiece of Irish drama. If these Greeks knew not Mr. O'Casey (how the devil could they?), O'Casey knows the Greeks, and hopes that the Republican Players will one of these days produce one of their works dealing with ancient gods and heroes. At present he himself is interested in men and women.

Mrs. Skeffington's statement that "every character connected with the Citizen Army is a coward and a slacker" is, to put it plainly, untrue. There isn't a coward in the play. Clitheroe falls in the fight. Does Mrs. Skeffington want him to do more? Brennan leaves the burning building when he can do nothing else; is she going to persist in her declaration that no man will try to leap away from a falling building? Will she still try to deny that in a man (even in the bravest) self-preservation is the first law? She may object to this, but, in fairness, she shouldn't blame me.

Langon, wounded in the belly, moans for surgical aid. Does she want me to make him gather a handful of his blood and murmur, "Thank God that this has been shed for Ireland"? I'm sorry, but I can't do this sort of thing.

She complains of the Covey calling sentences of The Voice, dope. Does she not understand that the Covey is a character part, and that he couldn't possibly say anything else without making the character ridiculous? Even the Greeks wouldn't do this. And it doesn't follow that an author agrees with everything his characters say. I happen to agree with this, however; but of these very words Jim Connolly himself said almost the same thing as the Covey.

The Tommies weren't represented without fear; but isn't it

natural that they should have been a little steadier than the Irish fighters? Mrs. Skeffington will not deny that the odds were terribly in their favour, and that they were comparatively safe. Sixty or more to one would make even a British Tommy feel safe.

The people that go to football matches are just as much a part of Ireland as those who go to Bodenstown, and it would be wise for the Republican Party to recognise this fact, unless they are determined to make of Ireland the terrible place of a land fit only for heroes to live in.

Sean O'Casey[15]

Mrs. Sheehy-Skeffington claimed to be speaking for those to whom 1916 was a national shrine, and no doubt she did articulate their feelings. It was inevitable, though, that a woman would look at the play through the eyes of a woman. Such a woman was Brigid O'Higgins. Although she felt the play had serious weaknesses, she saw that O'Casey was also a spokesman.

"THE PLOUGH AND THE STARS"

AS A WOMAN SAW IT

Sean O'Casey's powerful drama, *The Plough and the Stars,* is in the tradition of the great French and Russian realists, though it is nothing of a slavish imitation, for the dramatist is his own master. In this play, he gives a critical, cynical and impassioned picture of existence in the Dublin slums during the historic years of 1915-16. He does not shrink from portraying tenement life as he himself knew it, and if at very rare intervals the tragedy verges on melodrama—for O'Casey still lacks restraint—the man is honestly striving for the truth and is seldom very far from it.

Despite some palpable exaggerations which, when they appear, mar the artistry of the drama, and a certain looseness in construction, there is strength, sincerity and genius behind the work. It does not reach the same heights of dramatic intensity as its predecessor, *Juno and the Paycock*, nor does it touch the emotions so keenly—perhaps it is not so great a play—but there is a more terrible force, a more turbulent passion, a more ghastly Nemesis, which makes it more robust than the earlier tragedy.

In his delineation of character, O'Casey is most convincing. He attains less success in the kneading of incident into a dramatic whole. The characters in *The Plough and the Stars* are real men and women, and, while the dramatist is merciless in his depiction of these tenement dwellers, making no excuses for their shiftlessness, their inefficiency, there is nothing condescending in his treatment of them—rather is there a delicate touch, for too well O'Casey knows the pride of the poor. Throughout the drama the strength of the blood-tie is there. These people of the slums are his own kith and kin: he understands them, and, while castigating them, he loves them. It is this very love for his kind which causes his terrible cynicism and which gives the passion to his theme. Urged on by it, he must ease his heart and cry aloud of the starved, monotonous, wretched lives of these people—his cry reaches all of us who pass by the way.

What the result of this impassioned though cynical analysis of slum conditions in our city is likely to be is a debatable point. This at least the dramatist has achieved: by forcing us to face the facts of life as they are, the true, unpleasant things, Sean O'Casey has shaken our smugness; he has ruthlessly dispelled that convenient smoke-screen which would shut out from our comfortable drawing-rooms the awful reality of a side of Dublin life that men and women, our fellow-citizens, are daily up against. The dramatist has shown a remarkable courage in facing facts and a broad sympathy in his treatment of them. Perhaps he asks us to do the same?

So much for the artist's message! Sometimes an overemphasis hampers O'Casey in the artistry of its delivery. The lengthy well-polished speeches do not always sit easily on the lips of the men and the women one meets in *The Plough and the Stars*. The form of drama suffers somewhat from a lack of restraint. With regard to the handling of the matter, it might be remarked that it lacks cohesion, the incidents are isolated and need a linking up. Perhaps O'Casey overcrowds the canvas somewhat? But, realist before artist, he feels that if he is to present any full and faithful picture of the wretched lives of slum dwellers, he must work in incidents which are dramatically unconvincing, but without which no comprehensive account of existence in the tenements would be complete. For this reason he crowds in Rosie Redmond, the street girl, and little Mollser, the consumptive child. These characters are in no wise essential to the dramatic unity of the play—rather do they stand aloof, for neither knits herself into the heart of the tragedy. Ruthless in the presentation of facts, O'Casey philosophically accepts the first as an unpleasant reality and introduces the youthful victim of the white scourge so that her death may lend a deeper tone to the general gloom of the picture. Her frail body adds another corpse to the pitiful pile. Both these unfortunate girls find their place in the squalor and misery of the world Sean O'Casey knew, for it is not "the things that are beautiful, but the things that are" which are mirrored in *The Plough and the Stars*.

The introduction of the flag into the public-house in the second act of the play was an unhappy incident. Aesthetically it hurt. It was a crude stroke and hinted at a subconscious pandering to the melodramatic instinct which the author has not yet conquered. It is possible that what O'Casey stages may have occurred, but it is most improbable. Even so far back as 1915, the man, either in the Volunteers or in the Citizen Army, in charge of the flag, would be a picked soldier of reliable and trustworthy character, who might be depended upon to respect the emblem he marched under. Nationally, it irritates, for are we not still too close to the insurrection, still too near to its victory and its shadow to bear its being analysed in a critical manner? But for Sean O'Casey, the champion of the civilians, 1916 only meant war. He rages against all war, because of its terrible reaction on the lives of the people, more especially of the awful tragedies in its wake for women. Influenced by this view, he only sees one side of the 1916 rising, and he is out of sympathy with the higher one. O'Casey has missed the soul of the insurrection—a simple people's sublime act of faith in themselves and in their right to nationhood. There was a courage and a quality about it, which left him untouched. He probably viewed it as an ill-planned, ineffective military coup, which brought still more hardships to the already heart-broken people, still more wretchedness into the starkness and horror of life in the slums. To the dramatist who was socialist before nationalist, it was war, and war meant death and madness and terrible futility. But events have disproved this view, and, hopefully and patiently, Ireland awaits her golden-voiced poet to sing the story of glorious '16.

Though one may differ from the results which Mr. O'Casey has drawn from his critical and cynical analysis of the Easter rising, surely that is no excuse for the intolerance displayed at the Abbey Theatre on the first production of the drama. A dramatist is an artist primarily, neither a propagandist nor a politician. It is his right and his need to express his individual views on any subject which fires his imagination. Should his verdict wound our sensibilities, when are we, as a people, going to educate ourselves out of our touchiness? When is our impatience of criticism going to manifest itself in the production of constructive work? Let us meet the artist on his plane! Let us, above all, give him a fair chance to express his views, and when ours have crystallised into artistic shape, we shall expect the same courtesy from him.

In the meantime, those of us who are not fashioned in heroic mould are deeply indebted to the author of *The Plough and the Stars*, for he is the defender of the rights of the poor, the weak and the un-heroic. Nay, he is more than champion—he is friend. Good-natured Fluther, good, kindhearted Bessie, and poor little heartbroken Nora will never get beyond slumland, but in Mr. Sean O'Casey they have one who understands them, who thinks for them, and one also who, while he fights with them, loves them—yes, one who in a strange way respects them. To speak of these people and for them, to be the singer of the underworld—that is Mr. O'Casey's mission.

Brigid O'Higgins[16]

Ms. O'Higgins' analysis did not find universal agreement, but it prompted other women to write, and women, it seemed, had a different viewpoint from that of the men.

To the Editor of the *Irish Statesman*

Dear Sir,—Have you room for another letter on *The Plough and the Stars?*

Having so far sternly resisted all temptation to augment by ever so little the commotion caused by this intriguing play, Mrs. O'Higgins' article has determined my fall from grace. Not because she has sounded a note essentially different to the majority of those I have already heard on the subject, but because she has selected some features as being either superfluous or—with all due apologies to "Fluther"—derogatory, and which I believe on the contrary to be very strong points in the play.

First, there is the much-discussed incident of bringing the flag into the public-house. I cannot agree with Mrs. O'Higgins either that it was an unhappy incident, that it hurt aesthetically or even that it was technically inaccurate—the last point being immaterial; though I will allow that it may have hurt the sentiments of a few people and the sentimentality of many.

So far indeed from its being an unhappy incident, it seemed to me a singularly happy one—when viewed aesthetically, for it served no less a purpose than to crystallise momentarily humanity and its complexities. In discussing the play such considerations as the temperateness or otherwise of the Volunteers do not arise, and are moreover repugnant; it would appear necessary, however, to admit—that which no one disputes—that they were in the main temperate men, if not teetotallers: nevertheless, at some point all these men were human, and Sean O'Casey took the simplest, the most effective and, as it seems to me, artistically the boldest method of indicating this truth.

I cannot agree either that the introduction of the street girl and the consumptive child are superflous; they may not have knit themselves into the heart of the tragedy, it is true, but was it essential or even desirable that they should? Surely they were more real, more germane to the life which O'Casey depicts for us than the tragedy which overshadowed them; they are relatively permanent and afford, therefore, an unimpeachable background—aesthetically speaking, of course.

Here I would like to say, however, that I do not think the portrayal of Rosie Redmond was very convincing; one feels that such an inhabitant of that underworld would be rather more terrifying, too terrifying, perhaps for representation on any stage; and here, too, would seem to be my opportunity to record a fear that Mr. O'Casey is in danger of giving us a stage slum dweller, not too far removed in conception from the stage Irishman; the charwoman is perilously near this perpetration.

I feel I must dissent, too, with Mrs. O'Higgins' reading of the "artist's message"; chiefly because I cannot feel that he has any message. The people of the slums may be his own kith and kin, he may understand them, he may know them; but that he is "castigating" them, "loving" them or "easing his heart" of its fulness about them, I am gratefully not so sure.—Yours faithfully,

Kathleen O'Sullivan

To the Editor of the *Irish Statesman*

Dear Sir,—Arising out of the controversy on Mr. Sean O'Casey's play we seem to need an interpretation of the terms "Hero" and "Idealism." Mrs. K. O'Higgins, in her excellent article in a recent issue of your paper, says the author of *The Plough and the Stars* is the defender of the rights of the poor, the weak and the un-heroic. But surely Bessie Burgess is a true heroine. Surely the keynote of the play is that "one drop of the milk of kindness is worth more than the deepest draughts of the red wine of Idealism," such as Bernard Shaw describes in "The Perfect Wagnerity" as "Quackery Panacea." The person brought up on the panacea of duty may react to the panacea of love, and having found that also fail he may in the end realise that it is only the ability to stand up and carry on against whatever odds that really matters. We educated people of Ireland spend most of our time getting away from reality, and it is high time to clear our minds of cant and to try and see things as they are.

The heroic woman is supposed to sacrifice her sons gladly to a cause, as in *The Mother*, by Pearse. But is not the true mother more like Eve in *Back to Methuselah*, G. B. Shaw, who says: "There is enmity between woman, the creator, and man, the destroyer. It is long and hard and painful to create life, it is short and easy to steal the life others have made." In *The Singer* Pearse himself said: " 'Tis a pity of the women of the world," and "I seemed to see myself brought to die before a great crowd that stood cold and silent and there were some that cursed me in their hearts for having brought death into their houses. Sad dead faces seemed to reproach me. Oh, the wise sad faces of the dead and the keening of women rang in my ears." (Macdara).

Colm went out almost single-handed to his death more as a disappointed lover than as a hero. Even Macdara himself had been embittered by failure, had lost his Faith, and when God revealed Himself to him as suffering, loneliness, abjection, he courted death. He who goes on living for his country can also be heroic. Joan of Arc was killed while very young. Had she lived, she might have become an embittered and cynical female, out against people who refused to do as she wished. She was great because of her clearsighted commonsense, rather than from supernatural powers. Compare her "Voices" with the voice heard by Cain in *Back to Methuselah*. He says to Adam: "The voice does not speak to me as it does to you. A *man* does not listen and tremble in silence. He replies, he makes the Voice respect him, and in the end he dictates what the Voice shall say."

Finally, I agree with Mr. Lyle Donaghy when he says he believes all true ideals are practical. As much heroism is required in facing the daily fight against poverty, hunger and dirt as in attempting impossible things.—Yours faithfully,

A Seeker of Truth[17]

Ms. O'Higgins' review was followed by an even more acclamatory notice. The title of the article expressed the writer's sympathy:

THE PLOUGH AND THE STARS
THE PLAY OF THE SEASON

It is possible now, in the cold light of a fortnight after, to reduce to their essence the various emotions aroused by Sean O'Casey's new play, to separate their component parts and discover which predominated.

It is obvious that the intelligentsia is disappointed in "The Plough and the Stars." Concerned with construction and technique, as well as with the theme and characters of the play, this learned fraternity considers it inferior to "Juno", the author's previous success. After the intelligentsia come the Cranks; they disapprove of it not on any general grounds, but for individual reasons so diverse that it would be waste of space to catalogue them.

Finally, there is the most important person of all—the man in the street. The general public knows what appeals to it and what doesn't, without troubling to go into the whys and wherefores of the thing, and *it* has taken the play to its great heart. I have gone to some trouble to ascertain this. Five out of every six people I questioned about it had been so carried away by the play that they had lost all sense of judgement on it. The critic who wrote that the play would be a popular success prophesied right.

I wonder if the Abbey patrons have ever experienced such a thrill as on the first night of the "Plough and the Stars." The house had been booked out ten days in advance. On that night the streets adjacent to the theatre were parked with cars as far as the eye could see, and the vestibule swarmed with fashionable women wrapped in luxurious evening cloaks and men in "boiled" shirt fronts and dress clothes; and mingling with them the following of young men with large bow ties and mutton chops and ladies in extraordinary and colourful garments that form one of the aspects of the Abbey that we enjoy as much as the plays it presents. When they had sorted themselves out, rank and fashion and the State were allocated to the stalls and Art and Literature to the balcony, and the curtain arose on the first act, the scene, a room in a tenement house. During the act a man in a tweed suit, with a cap pulled down over his eyes, slipped into the back of the balcony and, leaning against the wall, followed his own play.

I can see why the critics hold that the "Plough and the Stars" is a less good play than "Juno." I thought with them myself until I went to see it a second time. Its absolute lack of form and plot is irritating. From the first scene the audience is waiting to be carried forward on a tide of plot, but is left with the sea of the real life that is depicted just lapping against it.

All the conventional ideas of what a play should be are outraged. It had come to see a play, and this was no play, but life sliced down with a merciless knife and dumped, slice by slice, before it, totally devoid of the butter and jam that would have made it palatable and covered up the crude materials of which it was made.

The play went straight to the heart of the public by reason of its sincerity and truth. Who has not at some time known an Uncle Peter, so delicious an object of laughter, so trying to live with? And the Covey; his counterpart is to be found not only in the slums, but in every parish in Ireland. I have known a village cobbler who was a Covey; and a farm labourer.

In spite of the thread of tragedy running through it in the person of Nora Clitheroe, the young wife who was a little too "grand" in her ideas for her lodgers and fellow-housemates, there are more laughs to the minute in the first act than in either of O'Casey's previous plays, and, dear, but it is good to be made laugh! But the curtain of this act brings one of the most tense moments in the play. It is led up to by the defiant confession wrenched from Nora by physical force on the part of her husband that she has burned a letter from General Connolly appointing Clitheroe a Commandant in the Citizen Army. Violently the husband flings her from him and goes forth to answer the call. It shocks us, this staging of physical force against a woman. It is one of the things we know happens day by day, but which we do not want to think about. We hate having our illusions shattered. We are cowards when it comes to having them questioned, and from beginning to end the play deals with them as relentlessly as an axe descending on matchwood. It is not in the violence, however, but the moment that follows it, in which the author rises to his greatest height. Nora Clitheroe is left alone, and a little girl with shrunken limbs and pettish suffering enters and begs to be allowed to remain because she is frightened to stay alone when her mother has gone to the meeting. The strains of "Tipperary" float in through the window as a company of Irish soldiers march off to the Great War, and the consumptive child, listening to it, and glancing at the deserted and broken Nora, demands of space if there is anyone left in the world with a "tither" of sense.

The second act takes place in a public house, and we see enacted what any of us who have the curiosity to peer through the open door of a public house, or through the window from the top of a tram, can see enacted any day, and hear if we have the courage to penetrate inside. I cannot for the life of me see why Rosie Redmond, in which Ria Mooney gave us a little gem of portraiture, should arouse the ire of some people who witnessed the play, and of a great many more who did not see it. Surely, they know that she is a feature of such public house life. If they do not, I can assure them, with my hand on my heart, that she is, and that she is an extremely good customer. I do not agree that Rosie Redmond had no connection with the rest of the play; on the contrary, she was employed to reveal the characters more completely of the Covey and "Fluther" Good, and the mental attitude of the barman. Without her that scene would have been incomplete. The author's treatment of her made her not only inoffensive, but it was so delicately and finely done that she left the stage leaving only chill horror in the audience. In treating that scene as he did, Sean O'Casey revealed himself a great artist. The most sensitive person might sit through it without fear of disedification, where a moderately thickskinned man leaves some of our variety theatres any night in the week with positive revulsion.

I have not the programme by me as I write, and I cannot remember her name, but I should like to refer to the exquisite little cameo of art given us by the actress who played the consumptive girl. Barry Fitzgerald, in the part of "Fluther" Good, had the part of his career, and was inimitable.

There are those who say that the agony was piled on too thickly in the last act. Perhaps so, yet it is eminently what might have happened in a slum tenement in one of the quarters around which the fighting centred in Easter Week. Out of the whole cast the figure which failed to convince was that of Nora Clitheroe. I do not think that a woman would have acted so in those circumstances, and especially not a woman who was supposed to be a cut above the tenement dweller. If Miss Richards had acted with a little more restraint, the part would have carried more conviction, and her voice spoiled it for most people, owing to her inability to assume the accent. I had rather have seen Miss Eileen Crowe in this part.

I wonder if any other author but Mr. O'Casey would have made Bessie Burgess revert to type and curse in her dying breath the mad girl, in trying to save whom she had been shot. There was something very terrible and real in the laboured, hissing virulence of the dying woman; in the sudden dread stillness of the house that knew nothing of respect for privacy, nor permitted escape from neighbourly attention, well-meant and otherwise.

I do not think for a moment that the author had any thought of propaganda, yet throughout the whole play, in little shafts here and there, is forced home to us the bitter facts he has learned from life—the infinite futility of war; the dread toll of the slums, as when the Covey, standing over the coffin of the dead consumptive girl, reminds the British soldier that more people die of consumption than are killed in war.

Unlike the vast majority of successful modern plays, there is no star part. It is not a play written for one man or one woman. True, there are minor roles, but the majority of the characters stand out separately and distinctly, and so form a fabric close to that of real life, in which only rarely one person is of dominant interest among a collection of people.

Miss Maureen Delaney gave us some excellent acting, but the laurels of the feminine cast went to Miss May Craig as Mrs. Grogan. I understand that Miss Crowe declined to play this part, as she objected to some of the lines, which the author refused to change. While being quite unable to see what she objected to, I feel grateful to her for the opportunity she gave us of seeing Miss May Craig in the part. Miss Crowe is an actress of talent, and I have a suspicion that, knowing better than anyone else what she can do and what she cannot, she realised that she was not suited to the part, and I applaud her commonsense in refusing it.

I have exhausted my space and have not said a "tither" of what I should like to say about this play, but I feel that if it may be less satisfactory, as a whole, the author has risen to greater heights than in "Juno" and the "Gunman".[18]

There were still nay-sayers. The "Talk of the Town" columnist of *Dublin Opinion* speculated on the unending possibilities of O'Casey's "realism."

THE TALK OF THE TOWN

We always write with restraint, and, therefore, we shall say that we found Mr. O'Casey's "Plough and the Stars" the reverse of the Curate's Egg—that is to say, rather decayed in spots.

Mr. O'Casey in his apologia claims the drama as "his place for expression." Would he express himself before a mixed audience in a drawing-room in some of the terms which he employed in the play under notice? Why, then, did he so express himself before our wives and mothers and sisters in the mixed audience of the Abbey Theatre?

Mr. O'Casey probably argues that people in real life use these expressions, and that it is his business to portray life as he sees and hears it. Workingmen in real life spit with vigour and freedom. Will Mr. O'Casey's labourers, in future plays, spit freely over the boards and possibly into the orchestra? "Real-life" tenements are never rose-gardens. Will our author's next stage-setting include a stench or two, in his determined effort to hold the mirror up to nature?

"Realists", we notice, have ever an itch to hold the mirror to the ugly side of Nature. It is, of course, within the power of any dramatist who cares for that sort of thing to create a sensation by dragging into the spotlight questionable, unhealthy and morbid aspects of life, and since, to the credit of dramatists in general, these aspects are not often so dragged in, plays which include them seem, to a certain type of mind, strong and original.

In the "Plough and the Stars" Mr. O'Casey gave us a real coffin. Next time, mayhap, he will go further and give us a real corpse. The "sensation" and the realism will undoubtedly be heightened. But is the thing really art and genius as Mr. Yeats thinks, or pretends to think? If it be, the heights are open to Mr. O'Casey.

Two of the most objectionable features of this play seemed

to us to have no other purpose than the creation of cheap and easy sensations. We refer to what appears to us to be the dragging into the drama by the hair of the character "Rosie Redmond" and the bringing of the Tricolour standards into the publichouse.

As a whole, the play is almost devoid of construction; simply four scenes from slum life during the 1916 Rising. It is conveniently and arbitrarily ended by the shooting of Bessie Burgess when possibly the author felt that the usual three hours period of entertainment was about up. It contains some good comedy (most of it in the first act with Fluther Good [and] the Forester harnessing for the fray), some vulgar horseplay (we allude to the fight between the women in the publichouse), some ordinary horseplay (the pantomime business with the pram in front of the tenement), and some of the most morbid and purposeless tragedy we have ever seen.

The performance of the Abbey Company is always so uniformly good that the acting calls for no comment. We must say, however, that we were genuinely sorry for Miss Ria Mooney, a little lady who, we hold, is potentially the finest actress the Abbey have [sic] had since we first became one of its regular patrons, and that is more years ago than we care to remember.

We wonder, *en passant*, what the "Plough and the Stars" would be like were the objectionable features (which are quite unnecessary to its skeleton of a plot) removed. We fancy Mr. O'Casey knows the answer, and that that is why they are there.[19]

Everybody had an opinion about what constituted an objectionable passage, but none expressed outrage as vehemently as a writer for the *Catholic Bulletin*—who resembled an O'Casey character come to life. Few reviewers matched this one for sheer determination to make a point. Ideas and accusations were spread over eight pages in an incoherent manner and ended only when, seemingly, he ran out of breath.

The points of contention for this writer were the Covey's line: "There's no such thing as an Irishman or Englishman, or a

German, or a Turk; we're all only human bein's"; the reviews by Walter Starkie and Stephen Gwynn; and an *Irish Times* editorial (all quoted above). In between, the writer attacked the Free State government subsidy to the Abbey, Yeats, Lady Gregory, and the Anglo-Irish Ascendancy.

After quoting liberally from Starkie's review and identifying him as a "Catholic product of an English Protestant Boarding School and of Trinity College," the writer launched into his tirade:

> So Easter Week, 1916, was "senseless": the ideas of the men of 1916 were "narrow nationalist ideas," and we are to *remember* the new word, "There's no such thing as an Irishman." Our authority for this is unexceptional: Mr. Starkie's words are clear: he is a favourable witness in every sense: he declares that the piece containing these remarkable doctrines, the play that is devised to "leave us at the end with *nothing but misery* in our hearts" is a play that "reaches the level of great tragedy: it rises up to tragedy on account of its human appeal." As a witness in the Subsidised Weekly to the Subsidised Directors of the Abbey Theatre as producers of drama, subsidised by the taxes of the Irish people, all leading up to the grand new doctrine, "*THERE'S NO SUCH THING AS AN IRISHMAN*," Mr. Starkie is most rightly placed, and is right worthy of attention. His views appeared in the [Horace] Plunkett Press [*Irish Statesman*] the morning after the Protest made in the name of men of 1916. Mr. Starkie has rightly defined the aim and purpose of this subsidised system of pouring scorn on the ideals of Easter Week, 1916. From the many utterances of repudiation we select one, addressed to the *Evening Herald*, the paper that both in its news columns and its editorial has the credit of having made a right-minded protest against this new specimen of New Ascendancy doctrine purveyed by the Board provided with a Director in Chief and Orator at Large in the person of W. B. Pollexfen [Yeats's mother, Susan's, maiden name] Yeats:

The reviewer then quoted, in full, the letter from Sean O'Shea (quoted above).

With Mr. Starkie's statement of the aim of the O'Casey drama we find that Mr. Stephen Gwynn, as correspondent of the Sunday Press of England, is in full accord. Warfare, "even when nationality is its plea," is all wrong. This thesis is now to be "illustrated," if you please, at a good round cost to the taxpayers of Ireland, "from Easter Week of 1916, which was the heroic period of the Irish insurrectionary movement."

The reviewer here quoted long passages from Gwynn's review of the play, written, as noted above, by "friends" and not by Gwynn; a fact noticed by the *Bulletin* reviewer. The writer ended his quote with the line: *"Since the subsidy, the Abbey has never looked back,"* from which he proceeded:

> Ah, *that subsidy*! There is "a crop of national realists" in the Abbey Directors, just as much as in the Sordid School of writers of books and plays: we have now not only a subsidised New Ascendancy linked up with the Associated Aesthetes and the Mutual Boosters, but we have the emergence of the New Nationalists in Ireland, with the watchword, "There's no such thing as an Irishman." But what of the Orator at Large, so unfeelingly depicted by the letter-writers quoted in Mr. Gwynn's weekly dispatch, as "a stiff, pompous, and furious Yeats"? We have devoted such attention to him as an eloquent Declaimer on Divorce and as a dreary Elocutionist on Education, that pains must be taken to preserve his precious words in his "stiff, pompous, and furious" style, as delivered unto us in the *Irish Times* of Friday, February 12, 1926:

The reviewer quoted from the mentioned paper the passages from "Speech by Senator Yeats" up to and including the paragraph heading, "Detectives Arrive."

> Of course they do: true to the ancient Abbey form. How else can an apotheosis be brought off? The wonder is that with the aid of another Senator (who is also "a wit and a poet," as Mr. Gwynn takes pains to record in the English

Sunday paper), Laurel Crowns were not available on the spot. They could have been handed out from the stage by the lady of the caste, whom Mr. Gwynn mercilessly describes—on the authority of his realistic correspondent—as having "shook a large fist at all." We have now recorded the deliverances of the House of Pollexfen on apotheosis: it is time to harken to the views of the House of Persse [Lady Gregory's maiden name]. The next issue of the *Irish Times* preserves them for us, in its account of the next performance of the New Nationalist drama, with its cry of "there is no nation: there is just humanity."

"The second act, toward which the opposition was most directed earlier in the week, was the greatest success of the night. Miss Ria Mooney's work was applauded vigorously, and at the fall of the curtain there was a demonstration of approval.
"Lady Gregory, who had journeyed from Galway yesterday, was present during the performance. She was fatigued, but very glad that she had seen what she described as 'a wonderful play, wonderful! wonderful! and O'Casey's play is humanity, humanity.' "

"Humanity, humanity," is the watchword of the Subsidised Stage, the New Nationalists, the Associated Aesthetes: "there's no such thing as an Irishman."
  The *Irish Times*, of course, could not miss such a very special opportunity of improving the occasion. The lead given by the Orator at Large in London, when in November 1925, he declared his intentions as to Education for Ireland, is splendidly seconded by the organ of the Ascendancy, New and Old. "O ye mere Irish, you are not educated," is its text, as it was the text of the Orator at Large, when he outlined his schemes for 1926 regarding our religious and cultural education. Hear, then, the *Irish Times* of February 13, 1926, to the same note:

The reviewer quoted a long passage from the first half of the *Times* editorial, "Cant and Facts" (quoted above), but emphasized with italics almost every other sentence, and continued:

> See how the Ascendancy organ plays, in every phrase, the true part of the Ascendancy: you mere Irish are not educated, not civilised—you of *Southern Ireland*, of course, are referred to. Herken to the true artists who deal with *Irish letters,* from Yeats to O'Casey. Understand that, *in this year of Grace*, when the Orator at Large and the *Irish Times* alike will advance from Divorce Diatribes to the Engineering of Education in the cause of the New Nationalism, you must get rid of cant. Even some of the distinguished audience at the Abbey . . . have to be warned against cant.

The reviewer quoted the last half of the editorial, again with the usual frequency of emphasis, commenting:

> Any attempt to deal with, say, the Sordid Swan Song of Senator Yeats, which rivalled, in the pages of *To-Morrow,* August, 1924, the performances of Mr. Lennox Robinson on the Madonna, in that great effort towards pre-eminence in putrescence, must be stamped on. It shows the "smug voice of cant," it merely feeds "the national vice of self-complacency." Allow this, and Diatribes on Divorce may become perilous. Moral censorship of the Press can only foster vice—national vice, too. The New Nationalists will soon dispose of these smug fellows. So the *Irish Times* sweeps on to the climax of its attack on Cant, and concludes with the note of its opening outburst, to the effect that "Our educational system, judged by results, is lamentable." Thus is the stage now set for the Houses of Pollexfen, Persse, and Plunkett, with all the Associated Aesthetics, with the watchword of the New Nationalism as their clarion call: "There's no such thing as an Irishman." Forward for "this year of Grace," 1926, O thou Orator at Large! Let it not be said again, even in the English Sunday Press, within an article by Mr. Stephen Gwynn, that "the curtain went up on a stiff, pompous, and furious Yeats." Truly your work is cut out for you, as the uneducated and uncivilised Southern Irish—vide the *Irish Times*—are wont to say. Educate the uncivilised: surely it will not be for nothing that you proclaimed to London, last November, how "Education is so running in my

head that I would speak badly of anything else." Thus is explained the Abbey Speech, so "stiff, pompous, and furious." It was not on Education. Give us "something more with the problems of life in it." Why not proceed to "get together *the right editors,* and they find *the right authors,* to *create a religious and secular culture*" among these mere Irish, who so lack education? Then there can be another Apotheosis of the Orator at Large. Let the more spacious stage be set therefor [*sic*]: let the Yogis, the Mahatmas, fashion new and nobler laurel crowns, in the name of New Nationalism.

The organ of the Mutual Boosters played up, of course, to its full form after the event. On February 20, 1926, it belauds this play of sorts, as being written "with a desperate sincerity," and jibes at the men of 1916 as "the idealists, knocking their magnificent heads against the stars." The sordid drama is declared to be likely to "do more to create *a true morality* and a profound political wisdom than all the sermons of last year": and it calls for "rural clubs" as "the true antitoxin" for the "crazes" of "our excitable people." The week that followed the protest has, however, added to our knowledge of how Orator Pollexfen Yeats expressed himself on the Abbey Stage. An unexceptional witness has come forward to describe Pompous Pollexfen on that scene. He was observed "to strut forward and cry with joy that the people of this country had 'been cut to the bone.' " With that witness's comment we conclude. "It is not a good thing that pompous fools should boast that we have been 'cut to the bone.' " We think it is a good thing: the New Ascendancy, the Associated Aesthetes, and the rest are welcome to expose their own natures. It will do good.[20]

After a torrent of verbal and proverbial water over and under the bridge and an exchange of bristling letters between the central protagonists, the stage was set for a potentially dramatic confrontation between O'Casey and Mrs. Sheehy-Skeffington: a debate. Some (including Mrs. Sheehy-Skeffington) doubted O'Casey's prowess as a public speaker. However, those who remembered him from the Labour Movement knew he was a superb orator. He had an astonishing knowledge of biblical parables and his Elizabethan spirit gave him a flair for the dramatic. Moreover, he had sat at the feet of the master orator James Larkin, his old friend and comrade from the Transport Workers' Union. His command of the English language was well known (as evidenced from the colorful dialogue of his plays) and he had worked long and hard to attain fluency in Gaelic. Years earlier, in fact, he had challenged a prominent columnist of the *Irish Worker* to a public debate, and his eagerness to take on the Irish Volunteers with polemics was still a sore point with many.

However, O'Casey's performance in the debate with Mrs. Sheehy-Skeffington was disappointing. The *Irish Independent* covered the confrontation:

"THE PLOUGH AND THE STARS"
AUTHOR REPLIES TO REPUBLICAN'S CHARGES
A PIQUANT DEBATE

There was a piquant development last night in the controversy over Mr. Sean O'Casey's play, "The Plough and the Stars," when the author and the leader of the Abbey opposition, Mrs. Sheehy-Skeffington, debated its merits.

Mrs. Sheehy-Skeffington contended that the play was a travesty of Easter Week, and that it concentrated on pettiness and squalor, unrelieved by a gleam of heroism.

Mr. O'Casey declared that Mrs. Sheehy-Skeffington saw everything through the eyes of a politician, and he through the eyes of a dramatist.

He also said he was not trying, and never would try, to write about heroes. He wrote only about the life he knew and the people he knew.

The dramatist and the leader of the opposition to the play met under the auspices of the Universities' Republican Club in the Mills' Hall, Merrion Row, last night, Prof. A. E. Clery presiding.

Lecturing on the controversy, Mrs. Sheehy-Skeffington said the main point of controversy turned on whether an audience had a right to express disapproval. Most authors and actors agreed that audiences had a right to express approval, and, therefore, the question was, whether an audience had a right to express disapproval by the usual method of hissing and boohing.

She thought that it was necessary that a protest should be made to hit the Abbey directorate in the eye.

There was no other way by which that could be done at present. "The Plough and the Stars" did not strike her as an anti-war play, but as an Anti-Easter week play.

Dealing with National Theatres, she personally regretted, not as a Republican, but as a lover of freedom and of the theatre, that the Abbey Theatre had been subsidised by the Government. It was now a "kept" house, "and any theatre lost more than the subsidy it received by giving up its freedom," and should in the natural course of events "kow tow" to the powers that be. Would it be possible in a subsidised theatre in Belfast for the Ulster Players to produce such a travesty as the "Plough and the Stars" of [Lord Edward] Carson's Volunteers before Sir James Craig and Lord Carson? Would not the theatre be wrecked by the indignant supporters of these two gentlemen?

"With regard to Mr. O'Casey," she continued, "my own impression of him is that he has 'a grouch.' He likes to see rather the meanness, the littleness, the squalor, the slum squabbles, the women barging each other, and the little vanities and jealousies of the Irish Citizen Army. He has rather the art of the photographer rather than the art of the dramatist.

"These scenes are all put together," and the natural conclusion is that this is a typical picture of the men of 1916.

"There is not a single gleam of heroism throughout 'The Plough and the Stars.'

"The theme of the play right through is the folly of it. That is why it cut to the bone, because we looked to see some of the heroism that did produce Easter Week."

The present Abbey motto was to see the squalor.

"I am sorry for Mr. O'Casey," she proceeded, "because I do realise that his plays have the mark of genius. He has taken

Easter Week for what is, after all, rather a comedy than a tragedy. We do wish that a dramatist will arise who will deal with what is great and fine in 1916" (hear, hear).

Mr. Sean O'Casey, who rose to propose a vote of thanks to the lecturer, only uttered a few sentences when he was overcome by a temporary weakness and had to sit down for a short period.

In the meantime Mr. Donaghy, a T.C.D. student, carried on the debate.

Mr. O'Casey resumed and said that Mrs. Sheehy-Skeffington saw everything through the eyes of a politician, while he saw most things through the eyes of a dramatist. She seemed to pay a great deal of attention to what England or America thought of them. He cared nothing for what these countries thought of Irishmen—even if they thought half of them were pookhas and the other half leprecauns.

Referring to the flag in the play, he said that it was not symbolical or representative of any one county or province, or of the Republicans, but was symbolical of the whole of Ireland, and if it represented the whole of Ireland it would have to take its place among the Bessie Burgesses, Jinnie Gogans, and Fluther Goods—even the Rosie Redmonds, as it did amongst the President of the Dail, the President of the Seanad, and President of a Republican convention. One of the golden stars on the tricolour was Easter Week, and in his opinion another was Irish drama. That flag had also to take the spots of disease, of hunger, hardship.

He was not trying, and never would try, to write about heroes. He could write only about the life he knew, and the people he knew.

"These people formed the bone and sinew, and ultimately," he believed, "they were going to be the brain of the country as well."

Mr. O'Casey then went on to reply in detail to the criticisms, and referring to the publichouse scene said that Mrs. Sheehy-Skeffington evidently wanted to bring everyone out of the publichouse.

Mrs. Sheehy-Skeffington—Hear, hear.

Mr. O'Casey—"I am anxious to bring everyone into the

publichouses to make them proper places of amusement and refreshment. The play, in my opinion, is the best of the three produced. It has been said I have been writing for England. I am not writing for England. I am writing for England as well as for Ireland, and I don't see why I should not.

" 'The Plough and the Stars' was handed in and passed for production long before there was a word of the London productions of 'Juno and the Paycock.' "

"All my plays were written for Dublin" (applause).

Referring to the critics, he said: "Do not mind the critics. No dependence can be placed on the critics. To my mind, the critics of England and Ireland, and particularly in Ireland, are the Bunsbys of the dramatic movement" (hear, hear).

Mrs. McCarville seconded the vote of thanks, and said that the play was an anti-Pearse play.

Mr. Gabriel Fallon spoke of the protest against the play as mob censorship.

Mr. E. O'Rahilly, Mr. F. H. O'Donnell, and Madam Gonne MacBride* also spoke.[21]

Holloway's account of the debate gave details not mentioned in the preceding article and alluded to O'Casey's method of speaking.

Monday, March 1 . . . I had tea with Eileen [?] before going on to Mills Hall to hear the discussion on O'Casey's play *The Plough and the Stars*. The hall was thronged. I arrived early and was seated before Tom Nally with whom I had a chat before proceedings began . . .T. C. Murray, Mrs. Despard, Maud Gonne MacBride, John Burke, Shelah Richards, Gabriel Fallon, F. J. McCormick, Arthur Shields, Ria Mooney, Joseph O'Reilly, Mrs. Tom Kettle . . . and many others I knew were present.

Arthur Clery was in the chair and opened the proceedings by merely introducing Mrs. Sheehy-Skeffington to the meeting. Sean O'Casey was received with applause as he walked up the aisle. Others were greeted similarly, especially the Abbey Players.

Mrs. Skeffington spoke mostly about the right to disapprove as well as approve in theatres, and was totally opposed to the police being brought in, and spoke most interestingly in soft, low, carrying tones. She is an easy, agreeable speaker and says what she wants to say clearly and well.

Sean O'Casey got up to propose the vote, and almost immediately felt unwell and broke down, and wished for some other speaker to address the meeting for the time being till he felt all right to proceed with his remarks. Mr. Donaghy stepped into the breach, and became quite eloquent for awhile, and then almost collapsed.

Then O'Casey came forward again, and in a speech put his point of view as a dramatist before the meeting, and then drifted into a sort of Salvationist address at a street corner. Then a young lady spoke and pitched into *Juno and the Paycock* as well as *The Plough and the Stars*, and quoted from a letter from Austin Clarke from London in which he said that plays that defiled the Irish were sure of success in London, or words to that effect. The son of the O'Rahilly spoke, and also Fallon and McCormick as to the position of the players. Fallon objected to the subsidy, the row, and the police equally, and McCormick said players should not be confounded with the roles they are cast for, as a player has to play the parts he is cast for to earn his daily bread.

O'Casey attacked a critic on the *Herald*, and Frank Hugh O'Donnell arose to defend the paper. O'Casey said he had no use for heroes in his plays, and Maud Gonne said she didn't see the play, but said he had no right to introduce a real hero—Padraic Pearse—into his play, and from O'Casey's own words could clearly see why the protest was made. Donaghy spoke again, and Mrs. Skeffington responded in a very subtle speech, full of sly thoughts and humour, and then the discussion concluded. It had been conducted in the most peaceful way and in the best of good humour, each taking or receiving hard hits in their turn.

The players made it clear that neither Miss Delany nor Miss Craig had been assaulted.

"Well, that is more than some of the protestors can say!" chipped in Mrs. Skeffington. She maintained that a protest was necessary from the nature of the play, and seeing that it would be used in London and America as Irish propaganda.

O'Casey said the script of his play, *The Plough and the Stars,* was in the hands of the Abbey before ever *Juno and the Paycock* was played in London. He didn't write for any stage in particular, but hoped for his play's success; he thought himself that *The Plough and the Stars* was his best play, but that was a matter of opinion. Fallon thought O'Casey the greatest dramatist Ireland ever produced. O'Casey thinks *The Plough and the Stars* an anti-war play, but, "If he meant it as such, his message escaped me," Mrs. Sheehy-Skeffington said.[22]

O'Casey's "breakdown" during the debate has been attributed to many things, not the least of which was that he was "gutless." Many years later, Gabriel Fallon, present at the debate, offered his observations. In his biography of O'Casey, Fallon wrote:

> Sean rose from his seat. His face was white and drawn and I noticed that he was attempting to shade his eyes from the light with his right hand. He began to speak—slowly, then hesitantly. I sensed what was wrong. He should have been wearing his cap. The peak of that cap was the only thing that could stand guard between his eyes and the light that penetrated them with agony. He stumbled in his speech; then paused. There was a tense silence. He spoke again. "I'm sorry" he said. "I'm . . . I'm not well . . . I can't . . . I can't go on."[23]

As has been shown in this book by references to O'Casey's complaints about his eyes, he was not well from at least 10 February, two days after opening night and at a time when most of Dublin was acclaiming his genius. Only a week before the debate, he referred to the continuous pain in his eyes and was under a doctor's orders to rest. It is to his credit that he continued to assert himself and to defend his play in spite of the pain and pressure.

Although everyone had his or her say, the issue was far from dead. The play was revived 3 May for one week, and more extreme measures were threatened. Yeats wrote to Olivia Shakespear shortly before:

> I have had a hint from an important republican that the anti-Casey republicans are going to blow up the Abbey the week after next when we revive *The Plough and the Stars*. We shall of course be well guarded but I shall not tell the company. Lennox knows and is seeing to the fire extinguishing apparatus. Nothing will happen but it shows the state of feeling. If we had not been warned, we might no doubt have been blown up as were certain Cinemas a couple of years ago. The man who warned me is certainly not a friend, rather the reverse.[24]

It would not be accurate to say that nothing happened, for as Joseph Holloway records, Mrs. Sheehy-Skeffington was still leading the protests:

> *Monday, May 3.* I met Mr. Meldon, and we were chatting about *The Plough and the Stars* when Mrs. Sheehy-Skeffington and a number of women bearing cards on sticks came along on their way to the Abbey. Meldon said, "A lot of that sort of thing is done for self-advertisement; the only way to effectively check a play's progress is to stay away if you don't approve of it. It is the box office that tells." . . . The ladies with placards stood at the kerb in front of both entrances to the theatre with policemen in numbers about, and Maud Gonne MacBride, Mrs. Despard, and Mrs. Skeffington in command. Kavanagh told me some stink bombs were to be exploded during the performance (and they were). Police were everywhere and were busy removing people from the pit and the balcony. . . . Many left the balcony after the stink bombs were thrown, and others in the audience commenced smoking and stood the stink; otherwise, though, it was in keeping with much they witnessed on the stage.
>
> *Saturday, May 8.* I went down to the Abbey with the intention of sitting out *The Plough and the Stars*, and stayed in the vestibule and saw the crowd go in. Three plain-clothesmen came in shortly before the performance began,

and two went into the stalls, and the man in charge spoke to me and queried, "Do you expect any trouble to-night?" And I replied, "I don't, but one can never tell." Then he spoke of the company being as real as the characters they played; it was a great company. "The actress who played 'Rosie Redmond' was the real thing!"

Then the play began, and on that instant the theatre became full of evil smelling fumes, and the attendants became excited. Lady Gregory had just gone in, and Yeats soon after arrived, and queried, "How are things going?" And he became gloomy on being told that the theatre was stink-bombed. He went in, but came back into the vestibule, where he wandered about like a lost soul.[25]

And so it ended—or at least quietly faded away. But Yeats was right; the news of the "happenings" did flash from country to country, and the world associated the *Plough*, as they did the *Playboy*, with rioting. Yet when the play was performed abroad, reactions were so mild that the Dublin protests were passed off as quaint diversions of the Fluther Goods and the Joxer Dalys.

In Ireland, neither the Left nor the Right—neither Socialists nor Nationalists—came to accept the play. Like Mrs. Sheehy-Skeffington, they saw the play through political rather than artistic eyes. Some cheered the Orator's sentiments, others applauded the Covey's; but few liked the play as a whole. In April 1966—the fiftieth anniversary of Easter Week—the play was not included in the official commemorative ceremonies. The bombing of Nelson's Pillar a month earlier was, perhaps, more than an object lesson.

And yet the play persevered. It was translated into at least sixteen languages, and millions around the world applauded it. It became the most popular play in Abbey Theatre history, being performed nearly a thousand times up to 1978. In 1976 the Abbey toured the United States to celebrate the play's fiftieth anniversary. Perhaps it was the Fluther Goods, the Captain Boyles and Joxer Dalys, the Bessie Burgesses, and even the Rosie Redmonds who made the play; perhaps it was these people who crowded the aisles year after year to watch in fascination their world on a stage.

As for O'Casey, Yeats was wrong. It was not his apotheosis. If anything it was the end of the beginning and time to go. O'Casey still had the majority of his plays to write, the better half of his life to live, and what may be known as his greatest feat to accomplish: his autobiographies. There would be more controversies: over the rejection of *The Silver Tassie* two years later; over the Boston banning of his play *Within the Gates* in 1934; over his politics and communism; over his continuing battle against what he saw as injustice and inhumanity. But for now, the disputes and arguments with some of the Abbey directors and players, the gap between himself and Easter Week, and the reaction to "my most ambitious play," *The Plough and the Stars*, had all taken their toll. Yes, it was time to go. There were new horizons to see, new plays to write, new techniques to try, and, though he did not know it then, a new Cathleen with whom to build a home and a family. It was time to go.

Notes

Chapter 1

1. *The Letters of Sean O'Casey,* vol. I, ed. David Krause (New York: Macmillan, 1975), pp. 113, 119.
2. *Lady Gregory's Journals,* ed. Lennox Robinson (New York: Macmillan, 1947), pp. 86-88.
3. Sean O'Casey, *The Plough and the Stars,* in *Three Plays* (New York: Macmillan, 1975), p. 179.
4. Bernard Shaw's *Man and Superman* was revived at the Abbey Theatre on 10 August 1925. After the performance O'Casey went backstage and told the actors what a poor production it was. An argument followed with Dolan and F. J. McCormick. For O'Casey's account, see the last two pages of "The Temple Entered," in Sean O'Casey, *Irishfallen, Fare Thee Well* (New York: Macmillan, 1949).
5. *Lady Gregory's Journals*, p. 88.
6. *Letters of Sean O'Casey*, pp. 144-45.
7. Ibid., pp. 146-47.
8. *Lady Gregory's Journals*, pp. 90-91.
9. Ibid., p. 87.
10. In 1899, Michael Cardinal Logue condemned Yeats's play *The Countess Cathleen* as heretical, even though he had not seen or read it.
11. In defiance of Dublin Castle, Yeats and Lady Gregory presented Shaw's play *The Shewing-Up of Blanco Posnet* at the Abbey in August 1909. The play had been banned in London by the Lord Chamberlain's office.
12. *Lady Gregory's Journals*, pp. 91-92.

110 Notes

13. *Letters of Sean O'Casey*, pp. 141-43.
14. *Lady Gregory's Journals*, pp. 94-95.
15. *Letters of Sean O'Casey*, pp. 165-66.
16. *Lady Gregory's Journals*, p. 95.
17. *Joseph Holloway's Abbey Theatre: A Selection from His Unpublished Journals* (Carbondale: Southern Illinois University Press, 1967), pp. 250-51.

Chapter 2

1. *Irish Times* (Dublin), 9 February 1926, p. 7.
2. *Irish Independent* (Dublin), 9 February 1926, p. 9.
3. *Holloway's Journals*, pp. 251-52.
4. Ibid., pp. 252-53.
5. *Letters of Sean O'Casey,* pp. 166-67.
6. *Holloway's Journals*, pp. 253-54.
7. Quoted in John W. Cunliffe, *Modern English Playwrights* (New York, 1927), pp. 245-46.
8. *Irish Times*, 12 February 1926, pp. 7-8.
9. *Holloway's Journals*, pp. 253-55.
10. *Observer* (London), 14 February 1926, p. 16.
11. *Evening Herald* (Dublin), 12 February 1926, p. 1.
12. *The Letters of W. B. Yeats*, ed. Alan Wade (London: Rupert Hart-Davis, 1954), p. 711.
13. *Irish Times*, 13 February 1926, p. 6.
14. *Irish Statesman* (Dublin), 13 February 1926, pp. 716-17.
15. *Voice of Labour* (Dublin), 13 February 1926, p. 4.
16. *Irish Independent,* 15, February 1926, p. 8.
17. Lady Gregory's Journals, pp. 95-99.

Chapter 3

1. *Irish Independent*, 15 February 1926, p. 8.
2. Ibid., 26 February 1926, p. 8. The last sentence was not published in the *Independent*. A corrected version appears in *Letters of Sean O'Casey*, pp. 168-71.
3. Ibid., 15 February 1926, p. 8.
4. *Lady Gregory's Journals*, pp. 99-100.
5. *Irish Statesman*, 20 February 1926, pp. 736-37.
6. Ibid., pp. 739-40.
7. Ibid., 27 February 1926, pp. 767-68.
8. Ibid., p. 768.
9. Ibid., 20 February 1926, p. 740.

10. Ibid., 6 March 1926, pp. 797-98.
11. *Voice of Labour*, 20 February 1926.
12. Ibid., 27 February 1926, p. 5.
13. *Letters of Sean O'Casey*, pp. 173-74.
14. Ibid., pp. 171-73.
15. Ibid., pp. 174-75.
16. *Irish Statesman,* 27 February 1926, pp. 770-71.
17. Ibid., 13 March 1926, pp. 11-12.
18. *Crystal* (Dublin), March 1926, pp. 47-48, 51.
19. *Dublin Opinion*, March 1926, p. 6.
20. *The Catholic Bulletin* (Dublin), March 1926, pp. 242-50.
21. *Irish Independent*, 2 March 1926.
22. *Holloway's Journals*, pp. 265-66.
23. Gabriel Fallon, *Sean O'Casey, The Man I Knew* (Boston: Little, Brown & Co., 1965), p. 96.
24. *Letters of W. B. Yeats,* p. 714.
25. *Holloway's Journals,* pp. 268-69.

Appendix: Biographical Notes

Allgood, Sara (1883-1950). One of the outstanding Abbey Theatre actresses who distinguished herself in the plays of Yeats, Lady Gregory, Synge, and O'Casey. The part of Bessie Burgess in *The Plough and the Stars* was written for her.

Barlow, Sean. Noted stage designer, scene painter, settings expert, and occasional Abbey Theatre actor. With the Abbey since its inception (1904).

Blythe, Ernest (1889-1975). Politician and theatre manager. Minister of Finance (1923), the only Northern Protestant to become a cabinet minister in the South. Devoted to the Irish language. O'Casey recruited him into the Irish Republican Brotherhood around 1904-5. Managing director of the Abbey Theatre (1941-67). As Minister of Finance he gave the Abbey its first government grant.

Breen, Dan (1894-1969). Republican and hero during the War of Independence (1918-22). Author of *My Fight for Irish Freedom* (1924). Later a close friend of O'Casey.

Clarke, Austin (1896-1974). Noted poet, dramatist, and novelist. Worked in England from 1921 to 1937, which included the time of O'Casey's play.

Craig, May (c. 1889-1972). Abbey Theatre actress who joined the company in 1916 and remained with them all her life.

Crowe, Eileen (1898-1978). Abbey Theatre actress. Married F. J. McCormick (1925).

Dolan, Michael J. (1884-1954). Actor and play director at the Abbey Theatre.

Donaghy, John Lyle (1902-1947). Poet and close friend of O'Casey.

Emmet, Robert (1778-1803). Leader of the 1803 Rising made famous by his speech from the dock at his trial.

Fagan, James Bernard (1873-1933). English playwright and producer. Responsible for many London productions of O'Casey's plays.

Fallon, Gabriel (1898-1980). Abbey Theatre actor and, later, a dramatic critic. A friend of O'Casey until his 1943 review of O'Casey's play *Red Roses for Me,* which ruptured the friendship. Author of *Sean O'Casey, The Man I Knew* (1965).

Fitzgerald, Barry (1888-1961). Famed Abbey Theatre actor and, later, Hollywood actor. One of the greatest comedy talents to tread a stage.

Gogarty, Oliver (1878-1957). Noted dramatist, poet, and physician. Senator (1922-36), Irish Free State. Called by Yeats "one of the great lyric poets of our age."

Gregory, Lady Augusta (1859-1932). First lady of the Abbey Theatre and the Irish dramatic movement.

Gwynn, Stephen (1864-1950). Writer, author of several historical, cultural, and literary books, studies, and reviews. Founding member, Irish Academy of Letters.

Higgins, F. R. (1896-1941). Poet, dramatist, and editor of several economic and literary journals. A director of the Abbey Theatre (from 1935).

Holloway, Joseph (1861-1944). Compulsive Dublin theatre-goer for fifty years and architect of the Abbey Theatre (1904). Attended every production put on by the Abbey and left his impressions of the experiences in a diary which covers 221 volumes.

Larkin, James (1876-1947). For several years the leading figure in the Irish labor movement. Founder of the Irish Transport and General Workers' Union (1909) and of the *Irish Worker* (1911-14). O'Casey's political mentor.

Macardle, Dorothy (1899-1958). Historian, novelist, and playwright. Author of *The Irish Republic* (1937), a flawed but monumental analysis of the 1916-22 period in Ireland.

McBride, Maud Gonne (1866-1953). Noted Irish revolutionary to whom Yeats proposed marriage (unsuccessfully). The leading actress in Yeats's play *Cathleen ni Houlihan.*

McCormick, F. J. (1891-1947). Arguably the greatest of all Abbey Theatre actors, known for his unusually wide range of roles.

Malone, Andrew E. For many years the dramatic critic for the *Irish Times.*

Murray, T. C. (1873-1959). Novelist and one of the leading playwrights for the Abbey Theatre.

O'Brien, George (1892-1973). Economist and for several years the government nominee on the Abbey Theatre board of directors.

O'Donnell, Frank Hugh (c.1894-1976). Dramatist. Not to be confused with the politician of the same name.

O'Flaherty, Liam (b. 1896). Novelist and short story writer.

Parnell, Charles Stewart (1846-1891). Politician whose affair with Kitty O'Shea made him a tragic symbol in Irish history. Founder of the Land League and a dominant force during his years as leader of the Irish Parliamentary Party.

Pearse, Patrick (1879-1916). Revolutionary, educationalist, and poet. First president of the short-lived Irish Republic founded by the Easter Rising in 1916. Executed by the British.

Richards, Shelah. Long-time Abbey Theatre actress.

Robinson, Lennox (1886-1958). Dramatist and director of plays. Manager of the Abbey Theatre (1910-23).

Sheehy-Skeffington, Hannah (1877-1946). Radical feminist and revolutionary. Founder of the Irish Women's Franchise League (1908) and active in the Easter Rising.

Starkie, Walter (1894-1976). Autobiographer, critic, and translator. Professor of language and literature, Trinity College (1926-43).

Tone, Theobald Wolfe (1763-1798). Founder of Irish republicanism and leader of the United Irishmen. Leader of the 1798 Rising for which he was executed.

Yeats, William Butler (1865-1939). Foremost poet of the English language, founder of the Abbey Theatre, and dramatist.

Suggestions for Further Reading

Although *The Plough and the Stars* is demonstrably one of O'Casey's most popular plays, there have been few worthwhile essays examining the disturbances surrounding its first production. Gabriel Fallon's sharply critical *Sean O'Casey, The Man I Knew* (1965) devotes many pages to it, and his is the view of one who witnessed the occasion.

In some ways the lack of essays on the disturbances is surprising since, like Synge's *Playboy*, the occasion and the riots are synonomous in the minds of theatregoers and students of the Irish theatre. On the other hand, however, this absence of writings is a tribute to the play's greatness. Its power and artistry have so challenged and intrigued the best literary minds of the century that the riots are, comparatively, a side issue.

However, one cannot adequately comprehend the reasons for the disturbances unless one understands the play. In this area there are several valuable essays which delineate the play's purpose, its merits, and its faults. Readers are urged to consult E. H. Mikhail's *Sean O'Casey: A Bibliography of Criticism* (1972) and his follow-up annual bibliographies in the *Sean O'Casey Review* (1975-80) and *An O'Casey Annual* (1982-present) for the definitive list of reviews and criticisms. Several essays deserve to be highly recommended. William Armstrong's "Source and Themes of the *Plough and the Stars*" in *Modern Drama* (December 1961) and Ronald Ayling's "Character Control and 'Alienation' in *The Plough and the Stars*" in *James Joyce Quarterly* (Fall 1970) are very different essays, but each gives excellent insights into the history and artistry of the play. Saros Cowasjee's article, "O'Casey Seen Through Holloway's Diary," in *Review of English Literature* (July 1965) is a good introduction to primary source material. The Spring 1976 number of the *Sean O'Casey Review* was a special issue commemorating the fiftieth anniversary of the play and featuring fifteen articles and letters which examined its various aspects. David Krause's article, "Some Truths and Jokes about the Easter Rising," in *Sean O'Casey Review* (Fall 1976), is an excellent examination of the mythology of the Rising and of O'Casey's attempts to humanize its participants.

Index

Abbey Theatre: Directors' debate over *Plough*, 13-16; financial difficulties, 6-7; government subsidy, 15, 96
AE (George William Russell), 72
Allgood, Sara, 17, 26, 28-29, 77, 113
Ann Kavanagh (Macardle), 37
Arms and the Man (Shaw), 60

Back to Methuselah (Shaw), 87-88
Blythe, Ernest, 27, 113
Breen, Dan, 37, 113

Cathleen ni Houlihan (Yeats), 58
Catholic Bulletin, 94-99
Clarke, Austin, 113; letter to *Irish Statesman*, 71, 104
Clery, Arthur, 103
Connolly, James, 50, 75
Corkery, Daniel, 5
Countess Cathleen (Yeats), 15, 44, 46
Craig, May, 17, 20, 23, 26, 113
Crowe, Eileen, 16, 17, 18, 19, 23, 113
Crystal (Dublin), 88-92

Delaney, Maureen, 16, 20, 23, 26, 29, 33
Dolan, Michael, 10, 24; on risk of producing *Plough*, 11
Donaghy, John Lyle, 62, 63, 113; letter to *Irish Statesman*, 68-69; takes part in public debate, 102, 104
Dublin Opinion, 93-94

Easter Rising (1916), 5, 9
Emmett, Robert, 67, 114
Evening Herald, 40-43

Fallon, Gabriel, 16, 17, 114; letter to *Irish Statesman*, 69-70; takes part in public debate, 103, 105
Fitzgerald, Barry, 16, 20, 23-24, 27, 30, 33, 91, 114; subject of kidnapping attempt, 56

Gaelic League, 5
Gogarty, Oliver St. John, 28, 114
Gorman, Eric, 24
Gregory, Lady Augusta, 114; on Abbey Directors' debate, 14-16;

initial reaction to *Plough*, 9-10;
reacts to protests, 53-56, 62-64;
on rehearsal, 17-18, 19; relates
Donaghy-Holloway discussion
on *Plough*, 63
Gwynn, Stephen, 114; review of
Plough, in London *Observer*,
38-40

Higgins, F. R., 27, 114; letter to
Irish Statesman, 71-72
Holloway, Joseph, 114; journal
excerpts regarding *Plough*, 20,
27-28, 36-38, 103-5, 106-7
Honor Bright, 38, 39
Hyde, Douglas, 5

Irish Independent, 24-27, 57-62
Irish Statesman, 46-50, 64-72, 82-88
Irish Times, 21-24, 32-36, 44-46
Irwin, Tommy: review of *Plough*
in *Voice of Labour*, 73-75

Juno and the Paycock (O'Casey):
compared to *Plough*, 20, 25, 26,
27, 50-51, 82, 92

Larkin, James, 5, 114
London Observer, 38-40

Macardle, Dorothy, 37, 114
MacBride, Maud Gonne, 103, 104, 114
McCormick, F. J., 17, 19, 24, 37, 60, 114
McCracken, Henry Joy, 67
Malone, Andrew E., 27, 114
Manchester Guardian, 30-31
Mooney, Ria, 16, 20, 23, 26, 33, 91, 103
Mother, The (Pearse), 87
Murray, T. C., 27, 114

O'Brien, George, 9, 16, 27, 37,
114; in Abbey Directors' debate,
10-15
O'Casey, Sean: illness, 64, 77,
105; letters to Sara Allgood, 29,
77; public debate with Hannah
Sheehy-Skeffington, 99-105;
relation with the ICA, 75-76;
receives applause for *Plough*,
27, 29, 53; *The Silver Tassie*,
108; threatens to withdraw
Plough, 17, 19; *Within the
Gates*, 108. See also *Juno and
the Paycock*; *Plough and the
Stars, The*
O'Donnell, Frank Hugh, 27, 29, 104, 115
O'Flaherty, Liam, 27, 65, 68, 69,
70, 115; letter to *Irish Statesman*, 66-68
O'Higgins, Brigid: review of
Plough in *Irish Statesman*, 82-85
Old Man, The (Macardle), 59

Palmer, Herbert E.: letter to *Irish
Statesman*, 69-70
Parnell, Charles Stewart, 5, 67, 115
Pearse, Patrick, 5, 42, 50, 104,
115; *The Mother*, 87; *The
Singer*, 88
*Playboy of the Western World,
The* (Synge): compared with
Plough, 3-6, 44, 107
Plough and the Stars, The: Abbey
Directors' debate over, 13-16;
accounts of disturbances during,
30, 32-35, 37, 38-39, 41, 63;
casting of, 16-17; compared
with *Juno and the Paycock*, 20,
25, 26, 27, 50-51, 82, 92; compared with *Playboy of the
Western World*, 3-6, 44, 107;

dress rehearsal, 20; historical perspective on, 107-8; moral debate over, 42, 84-85, 95; public debate on, 99-105
—Characters: Bessie Burgess (Maureen Delany), 12, 14, 17, 23, 26, 48, 49, 51, 85, 92; Captain Brennan, 51; The Covey, 48, 91, 92; Fluther Good (Barry Fitzgerald), 23-24, 27, 30, 48-49, 85, 91, 94; Jack Clitheroe (F. J. McCormick), 11, 15, 17, 23, 24, 26, 48, 90; Mollser (Kitty Curling), 23, 51, 84, 90; Mrs. Gogan (May Craig), 12, 18, 26, 49, 92; Nora Clitheroe (Shelah Richards), 11, 26, 29, 48, 51, 59, 85, 90, 91-92; Peter Flynn, 48; Rosie Redmond (Ria Mooney), 12, 13, 21, 23, 26, 28, 48, 49, 84, 91, 94
—Letters to the Editor: from Donaghy, 68-69; from Fallon, 69-70; from O'Casey (replies), 58-59, 80-82; from O'Flaherty, 65-68; from Palmer, 69-70; from Sheehy-Skeffington, 57-58, 77-80; from various other individuals, 61-62, 86-88
—Reviews: *Catholic Bulletin*, 94-99; *Crystal* (Dublin), 88-92; *Dublin Opinion*, 93-94 ("Talk of the Town"); *Evening Herald*, 40-43; *Irish Independent*, 24-27 (J.N.C.); *Irish Statesman*, 46-50 (Walter Starkie), 64-65 ("Spectator"), 82-85 (Brigid O'Higgins); *Irish Times*, 21, 24, 32-36, 44-46 (editorial); London *Observer*, 38-40 (Stephen Gwynn); *Manchester Guardian*, 30-31; *Voice of Labour*, 50-53, 73-75 (Tommy Irwin)

Richards, Shelah, 16, 20, 26, 29, 91, 103, 115
Robinson, Lennox, 9, 16, 17, 18, 20, 27, 115; in Abbey Directors' debate, 13-14
"Rosie Redmond's song," 10, 12, 15, 17

Sable and Gold, 59
Shakespear, Olivia, 106
Shaw, George Bernard, 15; *Arms and the Man*, 60; *Back to Methuselah*, 87-88
Sheehy-Skeffington, Hannah, 31, 37, 38, 39, 40, 60-61, 65, 80, 81, 82, 99, 115; letter to *Irish Independent*, 57-58; letter to *Voice of Labour*, 77-80; public debate with O'Casey, 99-105
Shields, Arthur, 24, 30, 64, 103
Silver Tassie, The (O'Casey), 108
Singer, The (Pearse), 88
Starkie, Walter, 95, 115; review of *Plough* in *Irish Statesman*, 46-50

Tone, Theobald Wolfe, 67, 115

Voice of Labour, 50-53, 73-75, 77-80

Within the Gates (O'Casey), 108

Yeats, William Butler, 18, 27, 31, 32, 40, 42, 54, 72, 74-75, 115; and Abbey Directors' debate, 13-14; *Cathleen ni Houlihan*, 58; *Countess Cathleen*, 15, 44, 46; letter to H.J.C. Grierson, 43; letter to Olivia Shakespear, 106; speech during performance of *Plough*, 31, 32, 34, 39, 41, 74-75, 98-99

About the Editor

ROBERT G. LOWERY is Editor-Publisher of the *Irish Literary Supplement* and *ACIS Newsletter*. Among his other published works are *Sean O'Casey's Autobiographies: An Annotated Index* (Greenwood Press, 1983); *An O'Casey Annual* (1-4); *"My Very Dear Sean," George Jean Nathan's Letters to Sean O'Casey; Sean O'Casey Centenary Essays* (co-edited with David Krause); and *Essays on Sean O'Casey's Autobiographies*.

OHIO UNIVERSITY LIBRARY
Please return this book as soon as you have finished with it. In order to avoid a fine it must be returned by the latest date stamped below. All books are subject to recall after two weeks or immediately if needed for reserve.

CF